Wondrous Stories

WONDROUS STORIES

An anthology of stories of Tzaddikim

With Commentary by

Rabbi Yitzchak Ginsburgh

Gal Einai

Jerusalem • New York

WONDROUS STORIES
Rabbi Yitzchak Ginsburgh

Edited by Itiel Giladi, Aviv Moyal, and Yehudah Haas
Contributing Editors: Shelli Karzen

Printed in the United States of America and Israel
First Edition

For information:

Israel: GAL EINAI
           PO Box 1015
           Kfar Chabad 60840
           tel. (in Israel): 1-700-700-966
           tel. (from abroad): 972-3-9608008
email: books@inner.org
Web: www.inner.org
Twitter: @RabbiGinsburgh

Printed with the support of
Ohavim Lihyot Yehudim אוהבים להיות יהודים ע"ר

Cover illustration: Zalman Kleinman and the Chassidic Art Institute

Layout and cover: David Hillel

ISBN: 978-965-532-068-8

בברכה להצלחה

"...It would be proper to publish your classes in book form.
With blessings for success..."

– from a letter from the Lubavitcher Rebbe
to the author, Elul 5741

Contents

FORWARD

This is a book of wondrous stories of *tzaddikim* (righteous individuals), as they were related by Rabbi Yitzchak Ginsburgh together with his deep insights into their inner dimensions. The inner dimension of the stories is like a key that unlocks their depths and embeds them in our hearts.

The third Rebbe of Chabad, the *Tzemach Tzedek,* said that stories of *tzaddikim* are the "written Torah" of Chassidut. Stories of *tzaddikim* purify our minds and hearts. They remind us that the world is not nature alone, but is also home to *tzaddikim*, wondrous events, miracles large and small, and Divine Providence. They highlight that it is God who is running the world. When we read a story about a *tzaddik*, we discover a person of flesh and blood who is living in a dimension that is inside the parameters of the natural world—but is simultaneously in the upper worlds, above nature as well. Sometimes the *tzaddik's* advice is supernatural and sometimes it seems down to earth. But it will always open us up to a matrix of clear and concise thinking, aligned with Divine reality. While the story may seem quite mundane, it is Divinely inspired, wondrous in its simplicity.

When we read stories of *tzaddikim*, we learn that we are living stories, as well. Rebbe Dovid of Lelov said that just as there is the Tractate of Bava Kama, so there will be a Tractate of Dovid of Lelov when Mashiach comes. One of the last verses of the Scroll of Esther says, "And the King Achashverosh imposed tax on the land and on the islands of the sea." The Kotzker Rebbe explained that this verse belongs to the next scroll." It is the inception of the next story.

If we understand that the world is a flow of stories and we too, are a story, we are inspired to live differently. The Midrash says that if Reuben would have known that his heroic effort to save Joseph would be recorded for posterity in the Torah, he would have picked Joseph up on his shoulders with great zeal and immediately brought him back to Jacob. If we are aware of what is happening around us, we will see the story. Reading stories of *tzaddikim* empowers us to understand that we have a role to play in this world. This is the true meaning of being woke to reality.

The Hebrew word for "story," *sippur* (ספור), is cognate to "sapphire (ספיר)." By telling stories of *tzaddikim,* we illuminate the spark of the *tzaddik* inside us—the root of pure faith. We are then saved from the impure husk of denial of the Torah and merit the resurrection of the dead.

The Alter Rebbe said that we should strive to "live with the times." In keeping with this directive, we have arranged the stories according to the day of passing of each *tzaddik.* This will help us to connect to them on the particular day that all the *tzaddik's* life-work is concentrated. With every year that passes, their souls ascend even higher. The day of passing, then, is the perfect time to contemplate the *tzaddik's* persona, to be inspired by them and to be empowered to live our lives by their ever-increasing light. We have included a short biography of each tzaddik at the beginning of the first story about him. The stories have been printed with a slightly darker background so that the reader will easily distinguish the story from Rabbi Ginsburgh's commentary that follows.

The stories and commentary in this volume were translated by Mrs. Shelli Karzen. The stories were originally written and edited by Rabbis Itiel Giladi, Aviv Moyal, and Yehudah Haas. They were first published in Rabbi Ginsburgh's weekly anthologies of teachings, Ve'abitah and Nifla'ot. Final English editorial work was done by Rabbi Moshe Genuth.

WONDER BOY: REBBE YISRAEL THE "YANUKA" OF STOLIN

Rebbe Yisrael of Stolin was born on the 10th of Kislev, 5629 (1869) to his father, the holy Rabbi Asher (the Second) of Stolin. His grandfather, the *"Beis Aharon"* said after his circumcision ceremony: "The Ba'al Shem Tov was named Yisrael, the Maggid of Kuzhnitz was called Yisrael and this baby is also called Yisrael." Afterward he groaned, "Oy, they grew up as orphans...." Indeed, when Rebbe Yisrael was only four and a half years old, his father passed away. Despite his young age, the *chassidim* saw him as their leader. He served as a chassidic Rebbe until he passed away on the second day of Tishrei, 5682 (1922).

* * *

The holy Rebbe Yisrael of Stolin was a Rebbe since he was a small child, and was called "the *Yanuka*" meaning "the child" (in Aramaic).

When he was no longer a very young Rebbe, he told the following story:

Once there was a very short bartender who was married to a tall woman. When he would want to talk to her, he would stand on a chair. Once he woke up in the middle of the night and saw that his legs reached the edge of the bed (because he mistakenly slept horizontally and not vertically). He thought that he had suddenly grown taller and began to cry, saying, "Until now, people would come here to see how I speak with my wife. Now that I have grown and will speak to her normally, who will come to see me and how will I make a living?"

* * *

The *Yanuka* was known for his "strange" and wondrous, childlike conduct. As a child, he performed many revealed wonders, but when he matured he stopped. The *chassidim* explained that as a child, the *Yanuka* had not yet learned to conceal his greatness. During his last years, he saw that there were many scoffers in his area and once again began performing miracles in order to strengthen the faith of his fellow Jews.

One example of a miracle that Rebbe Yisrael performed as a child was when a woman whose son's arms had been paralyzed since birth came to the Rebbe for a blessing. The Rebbe was still a child and enjoyed running back and forth. In order for him to hear what people were saying to him, his attendants would grab him and stand him up in a certain place. This is what they did when this woman came. "What is your wish?" the *Yanuka* asked the woman. When the woman showed him her paralyzed son, the *Yanuka* asked to bring him some rye (called *keychos*, which also means 'strength'). He then turned to the paralyzed boy and said, "Now I have *keychos* and I am giving it to you." Immediately following the

Rebbe's words, the boy stretched out his arms. He was cured!

Another story:

The *Yanuka* was the son-in-law of the holy Rebbe Dovid of Zlatipol, who was the son of the holy Rebbe Yochanan the founder of the Rachmastrivka dynasty. He lived in his father-in-law's home and he would do all sorts of things that would make him look rather impulsive. The sons of the holy Rabbi Yochanan spoke with their father and asked him to reprimand the *Yanuka* regarding his impulsive behavior. Rabbi Yochanan, answered, "I am sorry that I said something to him. If I would have known the magnitude of his intelligence and his broken heart over being an orphan, I would have been afraid to reprimand him."

The sons asked their father to reprimand the *Yanuka* after he opened the spigots of barrels in a wagon that was passing through the street, and water poured out everywhere. Immediately afterward, a fire broke out and all the places that had been doused with water did not go up in flames.

As opposed to the *Yanuka*, his contemporary, the *Sefat Emet* of Gur, was extremely organized. He is reported to have said that he knew what he would be doing in two years' time. Orderly conduct is typical of *tzaddikim* of the attribute of emet, or self-fulfillment (the inner dimension of the *sefirah* of foundation), which organizes everything. The childish conduct of the *Yanuka* is typical of a *tzaddik* who lives through the attribute of lowliness (the inner dimension of the *sefirah* of kingdom) and places himself in God's hands.

Archetypes of these two types of *tzaddikim* were Shamai (who was strict and meticulous) and Hillel (who was humble and flexible). Shamai would always buy whatever he saw in the market in honor of the upcoming Shabbat, exchanging it for an even better item if he would come upon it the next day. By contrast, Hillel would say, "Blessed is God every day." Today we will buy for today and God will surely provide us with the very best food in honor of Shabbat. Rabbi Yaakov Yosef of Polonne, the well-known disciple of the Ba'al Shem Tov and author of *Toldot Yaakov Yosef* explained that Shamai would perpetually rivet his thoughts to the World to Come, which is an aspect of Shabbat. Thus Shamai offered the adage, "Make Torah your habitual pursuit" (עֲשֵׂה תוֹרָתְךָ קֶבַע), since Torah represents that which is permanent and unchanging, like the holiness of the Shabbat. Hillel, on the other hand, always aspired to make a dwelling place for God in this lowly world, which is constantly changing. Thus, Hillel offered the adage, "Do not make your prayer habitual" (אַל תַּעַשׂ תְּפִלָּתְךָ קֶבַע), since prayer represents the fleeting nature of life and reacts to the changing circumstances around us. For Hillel, the actions we take in life should be responsive to the situations we encounter and be attuned to even the menial aspects of reality—such as heresy which also require a response.

The Rebbe Maharash: *Lechatchilah Ariber*—Leaping Over Obstacles as First Option

Rebbe Shmuel Schneerson, the Rebbe the Maharash, is the fourth Rebbe in the Chabad dynasty. He was born on the second of Iyar, 5594 (1834) – on the day of *tiferet* within *tiferet* in the Counting of the Omer – to his father, the third Lubavitcher Rebbe, the *Tzemach Tzedek* and his mother, Chaya Mushka. He was named after a hidden tzaddik, Reb Shmuel the water carrier from Polotzk. Despite the fact that he was the youngest of the *Tzemach Tzedek's* sons, he became the Rebbe after his father in Lubavitch, while most of his brothers became rebbes in other towns. The Maharash married his niece, Sterna, and after her passing, he married his cousin, Rebbetzin Rivkah.

The Maharash acted tirelessly for the Jews in Russia and the Jewish People as a whole, founding Jewish communities and lobbying the government for their needs. He coined the famous chassidic phrase, *"Lechatchilah ariber,"* saying, "The world thinks that when we can't go under an obstacle we have to leap over it from above. And I think that we have to leap over it from above in the first place *(Lechatchilah ariber)*. In the first place, we have to take strong action, not get sidetracked by anything and implement what we must implement. When we start in this way, the Holy One, Blessed Be He helps."

The Rebbe the Maharash is known for conducting his chassidic court with wealth and generosity. He passed away on the 13th of Tishrei, 5643 (1882) at the age of 48. He was laid to rest in the *ohel* of his father, the *Tzemach Tzedek*. His son, Rebbe Shalom Dov Ber, became the next Lubavitcher Rebbe.

A Torah Lesson with a Punch

Once a *chassid* entered the Maharash's study for a *yechidut* (private audience) with the Rebbe. The Rebbe asked him if they learn Chassidut in his town. The *chassid* answered that they have a regular class in Chassidut: every Saturday night, they make a *melaveh malkah* at the home of one of the *chassidim*, and they learn *Likutei Torah*. The *chassid* related that first, they prepare a big bowl of delicious punch and all the *chassidim* participate in the class with the punch generously ladled out for all. The Rebbe listened to the *chassid* and asked, "Do they really have to have the punch?" After all, punch is a luxury, a worldly desire. Surely the drink is strictly kosher, with all exacting care taken, but it is not something that *chassidim* generally do." Instead—the Rebbe advised—continue with the important study, of course, but don't include the punch.

The *chassid* unquestioningly accepted the Rebbe's advice and at the next class, punch was not served. When the *chassidim* asked why the punch was not on the menu, the *chassid* answered that the Rebbe did not see the punch in a positive light and advised not to serve it at the Torah classes.

The following week, *chassidim* still came to the class, but there were fewer of them. Gradually, the number of participants dwindled until the weekly class was cancelled due to lack of participants.

After some time, the same *chassid* came once again to the Rebbe and during the *yechidut*, the Rebbe asked him how the regular Torah class on Saturday nights was faring. The *chassid* told the Rebbe exactly what had happened: That since the punch was off the menu, the *chassidim* gradually stopped coming, until they were forced to cancel the gathering, altogether.

The Rebbe took this to heart and said—If the *chassidim* need punch in order to have desire to come to a class in Chassidut, then it is best that this should be done in the first place and not as an afterthought. Let them come to learn Chassidut. The *chassid* followed the Rebbe's advice and the Torah lesson with the punch was restored to its former popularity.

* * *

This is a story of doing something physical and pleasurable for a fellow Jew in order to ultimately bring him to do something spiritual, namely Torah study. Where do we learn that this order of things is correct? From Abraham, who hosted many guests. He would invite people to his tent to eat and drink, and then he would ask them to bless God. The Ba'al Shem Tov, too, taught that this is the proper way: First, provide a person with some material good, and only after that will the door be opened to draw him to some spiritual act.

The Rebbe the Maharash originally thought that the *chassidim* were already in an essential state of "mind ruling over the heart," with no physical desires, as in the Alter Rebbe's "That which is forbidden is forbidden, and that which is permissible—is unnecessary." (*Hayom Yom* 2 Adar 25)

This story evokes the directive of the Rambam in the preface to *Perek Chelek*, that one should give a child a candy so that he will want to learn (Torah), until the point that he will want to learn for the sake of learning.

Over the generations, we are all becoming more and more childlike. This is a common denominator for all—we have to get a candy and then we learn Torah. The Ba'al Shem Tov in *Keter Shem Tov* explains the inner logic of this in his explanation for the verse in Psalms (119:59): "I considered my plans and I returned my feet to your testaments." When we plan on doing a good deed, the evil inclination tries to prevent us from pursuing it. To silence the evil inclination, we have to give him his portion, a little bit of material pleasure ("I considered my plans"—*my* plans, i.e. for physical pleasure After the evil inclination has received its portion we can continue the pursuit of the good deed with no ulterior motive ("and I returned my feet to *Your*—God's—testaments.")

Answer a Good Question with the Real Question

The following story is especially good to tell to children:

Even as a little boy, the Rebbe the Maharash was blessed with great artistic talent. He would sculpt beautiful wood sculptures. Later in life, he was also an expert *sofer stam* (scribe). Some of the things that he penned and sculpted, truly wondrous works of art, were handed down from generation to generation of the coming Rebbes.

When the Maharash was five years old, he had a small pocketknife with which he would sculpt. This pocketknife was very dear to him. The adult *chassidim* saw that in addition to the holy books that he learned and his holy endeavors, the child—the Rebbe's youngest son—had a pocketknife that was very important to him. One of the *chassidim*, a wealthy merchant, had a pocketknife that was much better than the boy's knife. The *chassid* went over to the child, showed him his knife, and asked him if he wanted it. The Maharash of course answered that he did. "I will give it to you," said the *chassid*, "if you will correctly answer my question: Where can God be found?" The Maharash told the *chassid* that he would answer him, but that first, he had a question of his own. "Where can God not be found?" The *chassid*, who did not expect this answer, was silent for a moment and then held out the knife to the child, saying—"You won!"

* * *

How can we answer the *chassid*'s question? There are many possibilities: God is everywhere, God is in Heaven (as it says in the Talmud)—but the Maharash answered with a question: "Where can God *not* be found?" If you can tell me where God *cannot* be found, then I will tell you where He *can* be found.

The correct understanding is that God is in every place. If there is any question at all, it is the opposite question—Where can God *not* be found? There cannot be a place void of God. This elucidates the concept better than just saying that God is Above or even that He is in every place. By asking where God cannot be found, we structure a definition in our minds—that it is impossible for there to be a place without God, for if God is not there, then that place does not exist at all. Nothing can exist without God. This understanding, which in our story was perceived by a five-year-old, is the rectification of the *sefirah* of kingdom *(tikun hamalchut)*" which is the understanding that "no place is void of Him"—there can be no place where God is not present.

(It is interesting to note how the Rebbe the Maharash, even at the tender age of five, was already employing his adage, *"Lechatchilah ariber,"* leaping over the good question that he was asked with a far superior question.)

The Rebbe Maharash: God Before Me Always

Once a young married yeshiva student entered the Rebbe Maharash's room for *yechidut* (a private audience). He told the Rebbe that he does not love his wife and wants to divorce her. The Rebbe severely opposed the idea. He explained that it would not be good and it would even be forbidden to divorce his wife under the circumstances that he described. "It would be best to make peace and to continue to live in peace and love," the Rebbe told him.

Even though the young man was a *chassid*, he said to the Rebbe, "I cannot take it anymore, I cannot obey the Rebbe and I must divorce my wife."

The Rebbe became very emotional, arose to his full stature, fixed his eyes on the young man, and said, "Apparently, I do not have fear of Heaven. It is written in the Talmud that 'whoever has fear of Heaven, his words are accepted.' If you are not listening to me, apparently, I do not have enough fear of Heaven."

The Rebbe said these words with so much conviction that they penetrated deep into the young man's heart. "Fine, Rebbe," he answered, "I accept your words. I will not divorce my wife."

* * *

When a person has fear of Heaven, he is able to project it outward, influencing others. Sometimes, however—particularly if the issue is complex or difficult—"ordinary" fear of Heaven does not suffice. It is necessary to awaken the strong attribute of might and fear of Heaven in order to cause the listener to emerge from his self-centeredness and to become sensitive to God's Presence.

The Rebbe Maharash practiced this teaching not only outwardly, but even when he was alone:

The *chassidim* noticed that every time someone would enter the Rebbe Maharash's chamber for *yechidut,* he would take a special, large kerchief and place it on the table in a particular manner. The *chassidim* did not know why the Rebbe consistently did this. One daring *chassid* snuck into the Rebbe's room when the Rebbe did not see and lifted the kerchief from the table. Underneath was a parchment on which the words, "I set God before me always" were written. This parchment was always on the Rebbe's desk. When he was alone in his room, the parchment was open before him. (It is told that the Rebbe had another parchment with this saying in his glasses). When someone entered the room, the Rebbe would cover the parchment so that nobody would see.

* * *

From this story, we see how careful the Rebbe Maharash was to fulfill the first directive in the *Shulchan Aruch*, that a Jew should always keep in mind that God is standing over him. The directive, "I set God before me always" is written using God's Name, *Havayah*. This teaches us that God's standing over us is not to frighten us or make us feel disconcerted, for the Name *Havayah* is God's Name of compassion. In His mercy, God watches over every person at every moment. This is particularly true of the Rebbe, whose role is to arouse compassion on the Jewish people. He has to empower himself with the directive to set God before him always. The experience of constant sight—seeing Godliness before him always (beginning with constantly seeing the parchment before him) strengthens his fear of Heaven, thus ascertaining that his words will be accepted. This is all with great, true compassion over his flock. In the previous story, as well, the attribute of might from which the fear of Heaven stems was employed by the Rebbe in order to cause the *chassid* to act for his own true good—and was actually an act of compassion upon him and his household.

Rabbi YYB"Y of Ostra'ah and Rabbi Yaakov Yosef of Polna'ah: Anger and Consequences

Rabbi Yaakov Yosef of Ostra'ah (Ostroh), who was known as Rabbi Yeibi, (YYB"Y–Yaakov Yosef Ben Yehudah) was a rabbi and judge in Ostra'ah in Ukraine. His father, Rabbi Yehudah Leib was a rabbi in Ostra'ah and after his death, Rabbi Yeibi succeeded him. He was a disciple of the Maggid of Mezritch and founded the Ostra'ah chassidic dynasty, which continued until the Holocaust. He passed away on the 20th of Tishrei 5551 (1790), on the day of the Ushpizin of Joseph.

Rabbi Yaakov Yosef Katz of Polna'ah (Polonnoye) was known as the *'Ba'al Hatoladot'*, the author of the first book of chassidic teachings, *"Toldos Yaakov Yosef."* Before he became a disciple of the Ba'al Shem Tov, he was a rabbi and head of the Jewish court in the Podolia (Podole) region. There are many versions of the story of how he became a disciple of the Ba'al Shem Tov. He passed away on the 24th of Tishrei, 5542 (1781), and was buried in Polna'ah.

When the holy Rabbi Yeibi's father passed away, Rabbi Yeibi was only 17 years old. The holy rabbi of Polna'ah, Rabbi Yaakov Yosef, wanted to become the maggid (preacher) of the town in place of Rabbi Yeibi's father. He journeyed with his student, Rabbi Shimshon of Shpitocka (Shepertivka) to Rabbi Yeibi in Ostra'ah. "What is your wish?" Rabbi Yeibi asked them. The Rabbi of Polna'ah answered that he would like to be the maggid in the city. "The Zusman family heads the city," Rabbi Yeibi answered them. "If they agree, so it will be."

They all went to the Zusman family. "The Rabbi of Polna'ah wants you to agree for him to be a maggid here," said Rabbi Yeibi. The Zusmans did not want to make the decision and sent him to an ordinary Jew living in the city, saying that he would make the decision. They went to the Jew's home, where they found him lying in his bed and learning *mishnah*. "Yossel, what are you doing here?" the Jew asked Rabbi Yeibi. "The Rabbi of Polna'ah would like to be a maggid here," he answered. "And what do you want from me?" pressed the Jew. "Go to the Zusmans!"

"We were already there, and they told us to come to you," Rabbi Yeibi answered. "In that case," the Jew answered, I do not agree."

"Consider who you are starting up with," Rabbi Shimshon of Shpitovka said to the Jew. "With the Rabbi of Polna'ah. I am nothing compared to him and I am an expert in the entire Talmud."

"The chapter of *mishnah* that I am learning now is more important than your Talmud," the Jew retorted.

"I am an expert in both the Babylonian and Jerusalem Talmud, *Sifra* and *Sifri*," Rabbi Shimshon of Shpitovka countered.

"My chapter of *mishnah* is more beloved," the Jew retorted.

The Rabbi of Polna'ah and Rabbi Shimshon of Shpitovka left the city, and Rabbi Yeibi accompanied them in their wagon, with a second wagon traveling behind them to bring Rabbi Yeibi back to the city. The Rabbi of Polna'ah turned toward the city and wondered out loud, "Does Ostra'ah still exist?"

"You heard a decree from Heaven that said 'And Joseph was the leader of the land'" Rabbi Yeibi turned to the Rabbi of Polna'ah. You thought that was alluding to you, but you were wrong. It was referring to me. My name is also Joseph."

The Rabbi of Polna'ah immediately acknowledged this and said, "Of course, I made a mistake! I did not know that your name is Joseph. It is by law that you should become the maggid of Ostra'ah. Let us call the heads of the city and they will officially appoint you!"

Everyone came together and officially appointed the holy Rabbi Yeibi to be their maggid. The Rabbi of Polna'ah blessed him and returned to his home in Polna'ah. He then sent a glass chalice to Rabbi Yeibi as a gift.

The chalice was very dear to Rabbi Yeibi and he used it when making the ritual blessing on the wine (*kiddush*) on Shabbat. Once, on Simchat Torah, a bird landed on the set table and broke the chalice. When Rabbi Yeibi's daughter saw the chalice so beloved to her father broken, she fainted. When her father came home, he asked where his daughter was and they told him the entire story. He called for his daughter, and she came to the table in tears. "My daughter, why are you crying?" Rabbi Yeibi comforted her. "We will find a different chalice." When she saw that her father was not terribly upset, she was comforted.

Rabbi Yeibi told his assistant to find out if there were any merchants in town who were planning to journey to Berditchev immediately after the holiday. A merchant with immediate travel plans came before Rabbi Yeibi, who said to him, "The way from here to Berditchev goes through Polna'ah. I decree upon you that you should go to the Rabbi of Polna'ah and tell him that I ask after his welfare. Tell him, as well, that the chalice broke." The merchant promised and Rabbi Yeibi repeated his instructions three times, with a stern warning not to change any details.

The merchant set out with a wagon driver. After a short time, he felt exhausted and told the wagon driver to wake him when they would arrive in Polna'ah. The merchant woke after they were already quite a distance past Polna'ah. "Take me back to Polna'ah!" he directed the wagon driver, "and I will pay you well for the extra distance." "I am not returning to Polna'ah," the wagon driver said menacingly. The merchant felt that the wagon driver wanted to kill him and miraculously escaped from him and set out for Polna'ah. When he reached the city, he heard that the Rabbi of Polna'ah was critically ill. He came to the Rabbi's courtyard, which was full of men, women and children crying to God to save their leader.

The merchant did not know how he was going to fulfill Rabbi Yeibi's instructions under these unexpected circumstances. He began to call out, "Allow me to enter into the Rabbi's room, I have something that will heal him!" The merchant entered the rabbi's room and whispered in his ear, "Rabbi Yeibi asks after your welfare, and the chalice broke." Immediately the Rabbi of Polna'ah opened his eyes and said, "Thank God. The vessel has broken and we have escaped." (Based on a verse in Psalms). The Rabbi of Polna'ah slowly recuperated and lived a few more years.

The Ba'al Shem Tov had told the Rabbi of Polna'ah that he would pass away on the day after the Sukkot festival and that he would not pass away until he would be removed from his position as rabbi. The Rabbi of Polna'ah thought that it was virtually impossible that he would be removed from his position as rabbi, for who would dare to do so? When he became so ill on the day after Sukkot, he was sure that the Ba'al Shem Tov had been referring to this day, and he prepared himself to ascend to the upper worlds. But when he heard that the chalice had broken, he was happy that the decree was fulfilled on his chalice.

When the time actually did come for the Rabbi of Polna'ah to pass away, some simple workmen were walking under his window on Simchat Torah. They were drunk and were singing loudly. "What are you celebrating?" the Rabbi asked one of the drunkards. "Have you learned a great amount of Torah?"

"If I didn't learn, the honored Rabbi has learned, and if my brother is making a wedding, I will also take part in the celebration."

The Rabbi agreed with his words, and then the drunkard added, "If I am correct, I remove the honored rabbi from his position."

The Rabbi of Polna'ah became very frightened and when the drunkard turned to leave, the Rabbi said, "God will likewise break you forever, He will pick you up and pluck you out of your tent."[1] The drunkard died immediately. The Rabbi quickly finished up all loose ends on Simchat Torah, and when night fell, he called for the Burial Society, gave them instructions and passed away in great honor. May his merit protect us, amen.

* * *

The Rebbe of Polna'ah was known as a severe figure. He even discussed this with his rabbi, the Ba'al Shem Tov. Among other things, the Ba'al Shem Tov instructed him not to relay new insights into the Torah on a day during which he had become angry, as per the teaching of the Arizal that the soul of a person who becomes angry leaves him. The departure of the soul (*neshamah*) is also the departure of control (*shilton*—same numerical value as *neshamah*). This is expressed in the removal of the Rabbi from his position before his passing, as the sages say, "There is no control on the day of death." By association, we can also understand the advantage of the *mishna* (same letters as *neshamah*) that the Jew was learning with inner serenity, over the Talmud learned by the student of the Rabbi of Polna'ah.

The Rabbi of Polna'ah had a history of being removed from his position: He was rejected from filling the place of the Ba'al Shem Tov, even though he was the greatest of his disciples and the first to publish his teachings. Afterward, he was not accepted to become the Maggid of Ostra'ah and at the end of his life, was also distanced by the drunkard from the rabbinate of his own

---

1. Psalms 52:7.

city of Polna'ah. (The Jerusalem *tzaddik* Reb Usher Freund likewise used to say that before his death he would not be left with one follower…). It is certainly possible that his severity was the underlying cause—his trait of "left arm pushing away" caused him to be rejected.

There is, however, a second side to the anger coin. The Rabbi of Polna'ah and other *tzaddikim* employed the trait of anger as a tool in their service of God. "(People used to quote the Zohar, which says, "There is anger that is called blessed *(baruch)*" in reference to Rebbe Baruch of Mezhibuzh, who employed anger in his service of God. While anger is burning fire, it is sometimes better to critically contemplate life and "kill" it, than to create more and more new ideas that may go rancid. This is how we can also relate to the drunkard in this story. The Rabbi of Polna'ah used his anger against the drunkard (and fulfilled the verse in Psalms, "The *tzaddik* shall rejoice for he has seen revenge.") The Rabbi of Polna'ah elevated the drunkard's soul up to heaven with him, and in his merit, the drunkard reached heights that he would never have reached alone. The final chord of his life connected him to the *tzaddik* and the apparent revenge of the Rabbi of Polna'ah was actually a great favor to his soul.

The precious glass chalice that broke (the word for "glass" is זכוכית, equals תבונה, understanding) was an exchange for the passing of the Rabbi of Polna'ah. It alludes to the fact that the root of stringency is in the anger of Moses. Moses, who saw Divinity through a transparent pane, would be displeased when the Children of Israel could conduct themselves in an unworthy manner. The other prophets, by contrast, would only see the Divine through a translucent pane, like the silver chalice used by most people for the ritual blessing on the wine. When the Divine picture is slightly distorted in the prophet's eyes, he can understand why the sinners do not clearly see God's presence. The breaking of the glass in this story is like the breaking of the glass in the marriage ceremony. It provided the Rabbi of Polna'ah with another few years in this world, creating joy similar to a wedding celebration.

Bye-Bye-Bye: The 'Eshel Avraham' of Butchatch

Rebbe Avraham David Wohrman of Butchatch was a chassidic master, famous for his book, *Eshel Avraham*, on the *Shulchan Aruch*. The Eshel Avraham was a disciple of Rebbe Levi Yitzchak of Berditchev and Rebbe Moshe Leib of Sassov. From the age of twenty, he served as a rabbi. After the passing of his father-in-law, he was appointed to be the rabbi of Butchatch in Galicia. Rebbe Avraham David wrote many books on all facets of the Torah, including foundational books on the four parts of the Code of Jewish Law. He was also known for his deep knowledge of the exact and natural sciences. He passed away on the 29th of Tishrei 5601 (1840) and was buried in Butchatch.

The Eshel Avraham hardly slept or ate. He would pray at great length and he would learn Torah all night. He would also lead Melaveh Malkah festive meals (escorting the Shabbat out on Saturday nights) for his students and followers, which would last all night. One of the *tzaddikim* who was very close with the Eshel Avraham was Rebbe Meir of Premishlan (Peremyshliany), as depicted in the following story:

Once at the end of Shabbat, the students of Rebbe Meir of Premishlan brought him the wine cup over which to make *Havdalah* (the prayer at the end of Shabbat that formally separates Shabbat from the week). Rebbe Meir picked up the cup, looked at it, and put it back on the table. Once again he lifted the cup, looked at it and put it down and then repeated this a third time. Finally, he turned to his disciples and asked, "Who is the best and speediest horseman here?" One of the *chassidim* raised his hand and Rebbe Meir said to him: "Take the horse and ride out as you ordinarily would. As soon as you get out of the town, slap the horse three times (*"ein, tzvei drei"*) and you will immediately find yourself in Butchatch. The Rabbi there, the *Eshel Avraham*, holds *seudah shlishit* (the third Shabbat meal) for a very long time. Go immediately to his *Beit Midrash* (study hall) and you will see that he is still in the middle of *seudah shlishit*. Ask him what is the meaning of the acronym "Bye, bye, bye" (ב״י ב״י ב״י). As soon as he tells you, get back on your horse and leave Butchatch. Outside the city slap the horse three times and you will be back here. I will wait for you to make *Havdalah*.

The *chassid* did as the Rebbe told him and reached the *Eshel Avraham's Beit Midrash* in Butchatch in no time. When he entered, he told him that he was a messenger of Rebbe Meir of Premishlan and that he has a question from Rebbe Meir for the Rebbe: "What is the meaning of the acronym "Bye, bye, bye?" The *Eshel Avraham* immediately answered with confidence, *"Bnai Yishmael, Bnai Yishmael, Bnai Yishmael* (the sons of Yishmael)." The *chassid* heard the answer, got back on his horse and returned to Premishlan in no time. Rebbe Meir was waiting for him. When he saw the *chassid* and heard what the Rebbe of Butchatch had said, he smiled broadly, took the wine cup and made *Havdalah*.

Later, at the *Melaveh Malkah* meal, Rebbe Meir revealed what had transpired: "A very harsh decree had been decreed upon the people of Israel, and the entire Shabbat I tried with all my might to nullify the decree—to no avail. But in Heaven, they told me that if there would be another *tzaddik* who would join forces with me, together we could nullify the decree. The decree was on 'Bye', an acronym for *Bnai Yisrael* (the children of Israel). I sent the messenger to the *Eshel Avraham* who, in his wisdom, confidently interpreted the meaning as 'the sons of Yishmael, the sons of Yishmael, the sons of Yishmael.'"

That year, there was indeed a harsh decree on the sons of Yishmael, while all was good for the Jews.

The Eshel Avraham was born in the year 5531 (1770), one year before the passing of the Maggid of Mezritch. He passed away on the 29th of Tishrei, 5601 (1840), in his 70th year. There were many *tzaddikim,* including the Eshel Avraham, who, according to their understanding of the Zohar, thought that in the year 5600 the Mashiach would come and redeem the people of Israel. When 5600 passed and Mashiach did not come, the Eshel Avraham was so disappointed that he did not live for more than an additional month, the month of the holidays of Tishrei.

The *Eshel Avraham*'s passing after the holidays is reminiscent of his Rebbe, Rebbe Levi Yitzchak of Berditchev, who requested of God that He should allow him to complete the holiday season of Tishrei. His main service of God was in this month. God granted him his request, he completed the holiday of Sukkot and ascended to heaven on the 25th of Tishrei. The Eshel Avraham finished the month of Tishrei after the year that he anticipated would be the year of redemption. He died in his 70th year, similar to King David, the forbearer of the Mashiach.

Rebbe Yisrael of Ruzhin: Engraved on my Heart

The 3rd of Cheshvan is the *yahrzeit* of Rebbe Yisrael of Ruzhin (d. 5611 [1751]), the great-grandson of the Maggid of Mezritch. Rebbe Yisrael is commonly known as the Holy Rizhiner. Of all the pious leaders of his generation, it is known that he is the only one about whom the Alter Rebbe of Chabad said that he is worthy of becoming the Mashiach.

Rebbe Yisrael Friedman of Ruzhin became a leader at a young age and hundreds of thousands of *chassidim* flocked to his court. The most prominent—and definitely the most atypical—characteristic of his leadership was that he conducted himself like "royalty." His home was a palace, he rode in a magnificent carriage, kept a horse stable, used gold and silver vessels, and wore regal clothing—just like one of the greatest non-Jewish noblemen… This was also true of his behavior which was like that of a nobleman, with strict cleanliness, majestic splendor, and royal mannerisms and etiquette. Even his prayers, which some *tzaddikim* conducted stormily and with great fervor, were conducted in total silence. Indeed, this noble mannerism, in principle, is one that characterizes Rebbe Yisrael's descendants, the rebbes of Ruzhin, to this very day.

Once while traveling in the month of Elul, Rebbe Yisrael of Ruzhin met the *tzaddik* Rebbe Moshe Tzvi of Savaran, the chief disciple of Rebbe Levi Yitzchak of Berditchev—who was also on the road. The two *tzaddikim* were exceptionally good friends. They met near an inn, which was full and had no room for them. With nowhere to turn, each *tzaddik* removed a crate from his wagon and sat down. There, near the inn, they held an impromptu *farbrengen* between them.

The Ruzhiner asked Rebbe Moshe Tzvi, "How do you receive the many people who come to you for *Rosh Hashanah* and *Yom Kippur?*

"I examine them all together with one gaze," Rebbe Moshe Tzvi replied.

"But what do you do for them?" the Ruzhiner probed. "Examining them all at once is what is written about God, that the Children of Israel pass before Him like a flock of sheep."

Rebbe Moshe Tzvi turned to the Ruzhiner, "And what do you do? After all, many people come to you as well. So what do you do with them all on *Rosh Hashanah?*"

"On *Rosh Hashanah* eve many come to me: tens, hundreds, thousands, tens of thousands," the Ruzhiner replied. "I look at each individual and he looks at me, and he is engraved on my heart. When *Rosh Hashanah* arrives, particularly during the shofar blowing, but throughout the holy days, I open my heart to God. At the moment that I open my heart to God, all the notes and prayer requests from them all are given directly to God."

* * *

When a *chassid* comes to a Rebbe before *Rosh Hashanah,* he writes a *pidyon nefesh*—a note with his request. In the court of the Lubavitcher Rebbe, for example, the Rebbe would bring huge bags full of thousands of these notes to the shofar blowing. He would cover himself with his prayer shawl and cry profusely before the shofar blowing, in order to awaken Divine compassion on all the people who had requested his blessing.

The Rebbe of Ruzhin had a different method: He did not request notes. Instead, he wanted to see each person. Then the person and his note would be engraved on his heart. When *Rosh Hashanah* would come, he would simply open his heart to God and then all the notes would be given directly to the Master of the Universe. This was *Rosh Hashanah* with the Ruzhiner.

The Ruzhiner also related that when a person filled with sins would come to him, he himself would repent for all of his own sins, and then the gates of repentance would be opened for all. In Kabbalah, it is written that the persona of *Imma*—whose inner dimension is the act of repentance, extends down (through its foundation) until beauty (*tiferet*) in the emotive attributes. The heart of the *tzaddik* is his attribute of *tiferet,* the *tiferet* of Israel (the name of Rebbe Israel of Ruzhin, who was named after the Ba'al Shem Tov) in which all the souls of Israel are included. Every person who has the merit to meet a true *tzaddik* is engraved on his heart, on his attribute of *tiferet*—and the *tzaddik* does not have to explicitly mention him in his prayers in order to bring Divine abundance upon him.

When we merit to meet a true *tzaddik,* we are engraved upon his heart, which opens the gates of repentance for us and brings Divine abundance down to us, as all souls are included in his heart. And then we are inscribed for a good and sweet year in both the physical and spiritual realms.

Rebbe Nachum of Chernobyl: Is the World Refined Enough to Turn Evil to Ashes?

Rebbe Menachem Nachum of Chernobyl (also known by the title of his book, the *Ma'or Einayim*) founded the chassidic dynasty of Chernobyl. He was the eldest of the disciples of the Maggid of Mezritch and even had the merit to learn directly from the Ba'al Shem Tov, himself. According to the Lubavitcher Rebbe, Rebbe Nachum was the grandson of Rabbi Adam Ba'al Shem.

Rebbe Nachum traveled from Jewish town to Jewish town to awaken the people to follow the path of ethics and Chassidut. After the passing of his mentor, the Maggid of Mezritch, many *chassidim* saw Rebbe Nachum as his successor, and Rebbe Nachum became a chassidic rebbe. He established his court in a number of places until it settled permanently in Chernobyl (Ukraine).

Among Rebbe Nachum's disciples were the *Bat Ayin* (Rebbe Avraham Dov of Avritch) and his son, Rebbe Mordechai of Chernobyl. His famous book, *Ma'or Einayim*, is one of the fundamental books of Chassidut. Additional chassidic sects that stemmed from the Chernobyl court are Tulna, Skver and Rachamstrivska (Rachmistroika).

Rebbe Nachum passed away on the 11th of Cheshvan and was laid to rest in Chernobyl.

There were two situations in which Rebbe Nachum of Chernobyl would act with special self-sacrifice: Redemption of captives (like many of the disciples of the Ba'al Shem Tov) and spiritually helping women in the throes of a difficult childbirth.

Once, a case of a particular woman in the midst of a most difficult birth was brought before Rebbe Nachum. She was literally in danger of death. Rebbe Nachum had *ruach hakodesh* (Divine inspiration) and saw that he could not help this woman. He did not have the power to hasten the birth.

Just as nowadays, there are technical methods to hasten a birth, a *tzaddik* has his own methods—a special power to inject spiritual power to hasten a birth. In the case of this woman, Rebbe Nachum felt that he did not have the power to help. As Rebbe Nachum was contemplating this sorry state of affairs—and of course, feeling sorrow to the depths of his soul, for this was one of his personal areas of self-sacrifice—a messenger ran into Rebbe Nachum's study hall and happily announced that the woman had given birth to a son, in good health.

Rebbe Nachum joined in the hearty rounds of *mazal tov*. But inside, he was perplexed. After all, he had seen with his *ruach hakodesh* that this was a lost cause Thus, he found it difficult to understand how this woman gave birth in good health. Rebbe Nachum began to ask exactly what had transpired.

This woman did not live in Chernobyl, but rather, in a nearby village. The people present told Rebbe Nachum that in that village, there lived an elderly non-Jew who would give medicines and charms for all sorts of situations. When the people caring for this woman saw her desperate situation, they called the elderly non-Jew, and his medicine immediately worked.

"I must meet this old man," said Rebbe Nachum. "I also have charms, but this time they did not work. I want to meet this man and discover the source of his power."

Rebbe Nachum went to meet the old man, who received the rabbi cordially.

"What is the source of your power?" asked Rebbe Nachum. Where did you learn to make these medicines and charms?"

The old man answered directly. "I am connected to powers of impurity, demons and spirits and I learned my profession from them.

"I would also like to learn this profession," Rebbe Nachum said. "Can you take me to your mentors?"

The old man agreed and led Rebbe Nachum to a certain place in the field, where they sat and waited. After some time, a cat with two tails suddenly came out of a hole. The Rebbe and the old man looked at the two-tailed cat for a few seconds and suddenly Rebbe Nachum heard a booming voice from heaven commanding him, "Bow down to the cat!" As soon as he heard that, Rebbe Nachum shouted with all his might, *"Shema Yisrael, Hashem Elokeinu Hashem Echad!"* (Hear O' Israel, *Havayah* is our God, *Havayah* is One). The cat evaporated into thin air and the entire area, which was full of spirits, demons and impure forces, quaked.

Rebbe Nachum did not want to harm the old man. "Let us leave quickly," he told him, "before I obliterate the entire reality in this valley."

A Good-Good Jew and a Good-Bad Jew

This story was told by one of the great *tzaddikim* of that generation, Rebbe Baruch of Mezhibuzh, who was the Ba'al Shem Tov's grandson. Rebbe Baruch was also a very good friend of Rebbe Nachum's. When Rebbe Baruch would tell this story, he would end it by saying, "If I had been there, I would have turned them into ash. I wouldn't have sufficed with the disappearance of the cat and the quaking and then left. I would have turned the entire area into ashes."

Why didn't Rebbe Nachum, whose power was certainly as great as Rebbe Baruch's, turn everything into ash? Why was he content with a minor earthquake and then quickly left, "before he would obliterate the entire area?"

Apparently, Rebbe Nachum understood that the time was not yet ripe for the complete fulfillment of the verse, "And the spirit of impurity, I will remove from the land."[1] The elimination of the spirit of impurity is one of the signs of the redemption and it is also one of the signs of our generation—things for which the time was not yet ripe in previous generations have now matured and their time has arrived.

All the *tzaddikim* who were disciples of the Ba'al Shem Tov—except for those in the Chabad tradition—were called "a *guter yid*" (a good Jew). When Rebbe Baruch of Mezhibuzh spoke about his friend Rebbe Nachum, he depicted the difference between them, saying, "I am a *beizer gutter* Yid (a good bad Jew) and Rebbe Nachum is a *guter guter* Yid (a good, good Jew). In other words, one can be a good, good Jew, and one can be a good, bad Jew—bad toward those who deserve to be related to in this way—employing the attribute of might to rectify them.

The good bad Jew would have turned them into ash, but the

---

1.   *Zechariah* 13:2.

good, good Jew just caused a shake-up and temporary nulli-fication of the impurity. Until the Mashiach comes, however, that reality still needs rectification.

The Matriarch Rachel: The Root of Salvation for Difficult Childbirth

The 11th of Cheshvan is also the day of passing of the Matriarch Rachel, who died in childbirth. Why was her husband Jacob unable to employ some spiritual power to help her? Was he less powerful than the Ba'al Shem Tov and all the *tzaddikim* who knew how to arouse mercy on women in difficult childbirth?

First, sometimes, it is necessary for someone to volunteer to actually sacrifice his or her soul so that afterward, it will be possible to save tens of thousands of similar cases. The power of Rachel's self-sacrifice gave power to the *tzaddikim* in all the generations to help women in difficult childbirth.

In addition, the world is becoming more and more refined from generation to generation. We are all aware of the concept called, "the descent of the generations." But, just as there is deterioration of the generations, there is also the concept called *tikkun olam*, "the rectification of the world" a process that is slowly taking place in preparation for the final redemption.

There were many things that could not be done prior to the Giving of the Torah, which subsequently became possible. The patriarchs and matriarchs lived before the Giving of the Torah. Souls as great as theirs almost did not exist afterward (except for Moses and a few other individuals). Nonetheless, the power of the Giving of the Torah gave humanity boldness and the power to take action in ways that the holy patriarchs could not. This is because the world is progressing and becoming more refined.

The core event that propelled the world forward was the

Giving of the Torah, but in every generation, the energy from that event can be drawn down ever more, since: "Every day they should be new in your eyes,"[2]—literally new. The Giving of the Torah and progress toward Mashiach takes place in every generation—even though thousands of years have passed. This is why there are things that are possible today, that would have been impossible in the past. Even in external reality, in technology, for example, there is progress all the time. Just as there are new innovations today that did not exist previously in external reality, the spiritual realm is progressing as well.

____

2.   *Shulchan Aruch Orach Chaim* 61.

Rabbi Menachem Mendel Hager of Kosov: Expanded Consciousness in the Land of Israel

Rebbe Menachem Mendel Hager of Kosov, known for his famous book, *Ahavat Shalom,* was the patriarch of the Kosov-Vizhnitz dynasty. He was born to his father, Rabbi Yaakov Kapil, adisciple of the Ba'al Shem Tov and the regular prayer leader in his study hall. Rebbe Menachem Mendel was a disciple of Rebbe Ze'ev Wolf of Cherniostra, Rebbe Moshe Leib of Sassov, Rebbe Meshulam Feivush of Zhebrizh and Rebbe Tzvi Hirsch of Nadvorna. Rebbe Menachem Mendel—and his entire dynasty after him—was famous for his extraordinary love of Israel. The Seer of Lublin said that Rebbe Menachem Mendel was the "king of Israel."

Rebbe Menachem Mendel passed away on the 17th of Cheshvan, 5586 (1825) and was laid to rest in Kosov. His son, Rebbe Chaim, succeeded him.

When the holy Rabbi Ze'ev Wolf of Cherniostra was on his way to making *aliyah* to the land of Israel, he sent one of his students to Kosov, to his disciple, the holy Rebbe Menachem Mendel. Rabbi Ze'ev instructed his messenger to tell Rebbe Menachem Mendel in his name that he hereby ordains him to be a Rebbe and leader of the Jewish people.

At that time, Rebbe Menachem Mendel was extremely poor. He and his family lived in dire poverty. To earn their scant income, his wife would sell a certain type of plaster. (She would heat up bricks and then cool them in cold water. The bricks would melt and turn into plaster). This was extremely hard work, but it was her way of eking out a meager living for her family. When Rebbe Ze'ev's messenger arrived at their home, he saw the Rebbetzin in the yard with their pot of plaster. The children were running in the yard and inadvertently kicked over all the barrels of plaster. The contents of the barrels poured out onto the ground and all of the Rebbetzin's hard work and potential to put a bit of food on the table were ruined.

Upset, the Rebbetzin entered her holy husband's room. He was sitting and learning Torah. "Look what your children have done," cried the Rebbetzin. Rebbe Menachem Mendel calmly answered, "When the situation gets so bad, it is a sign that all will be good." While they were still speaking, Rebbe Ze'ev's messenger came in and announced, "The Rebbe has sent me to tell you that it is already fine for you to become a Rebbe."

The messenger left immediately and a Jew entered Rebbe Menachem Mendel's home and gave him a note asking for a blessing, along with a large sum of money, which covered all of Rebbe Menachem Mendel's needs. We see here that his words, "When the situation gets so bad, it is a sign that all will be good," were immediately fulfilled.

When the holy Rabbi of Cherni-Ostra'ah arrived in the Holy Land, he wrote a letter to his disciple, Rebbe Menachem Mendel of Kosov, as follows: *"Today is Sunday, yesterday we blessed the new month of Sivan. May his kingdom* (addressing Rebbe Menachem Mendel in the third person was a sign of respect) *be renewed upon himself and all his household and never leave him and his sons and his descendants from now and forever…"*

While there are great *tzaddikim* whose descendants do not succeed them, Rebbe Menachem Mendel's Vizhnitz dynasty has continued on to this very day.

All of the stages in this story are a reflection of the *mochin* (intellectual prowess) of the Land of Israel. Although Rebbe Ze'ev Wolf could have blessed Rebbe Menachem Mendel with continuity when he was still in Poland, or sent him the message with the messenger when he ordained him as a rabbi, he chose to do so specifically when he arrived in the Land of Israel. It is in the Land of Israel that he saw that his disciple, Rebbe Menachem Mendel, would remain a rebbe, as would his successors throughout the coming generations.

Ordainment to become a rabbi was given to Rebbe Menachem Mendel specifically by a messenger, while Rabbi Ze'ev Wolf was on his way to the Land of Israel. The Ba'al Shem Tov taught that "a person is where his thoughts are." As Rabbi Ze'ev Wolf's thoughts at that point were immersed in the Land of Israel, he was already privy to the inspiration of the Land and knew who would succeed him. (In Chabad, too the Alter Rebbe was appointed to his position of Rebbe by his own teacher, Rebbe Menachem Mendel of Vitebsk when the latter was on his way to the Land of Israel). By contrast, Rebbe Ze'ev Wolf wrote the promise of continuity in his own handwriting when he was already physically in the Land of Israel.

Every *tzaddik* in the diaspora has the *mochin* (intellectual prowess) of the Land of Israel at all times, but they are in a state of pregnancy, corresponding to the behavioral attributes of the soul. When he goes to the Land of Israel, the *tzaddik* receives the *mochin* of a young child, corresponding to the emotional attributes of the soul. And when the *tzaddik* actually lives in the Land of Israel, he receives the *mochin* of the Land of Israel, corresponding to the expanded consciousness of the intellectual attributes of the soul (wisdom, understanding and knowledge). It is specifically from the expanded consciousness of the Land of Israel that the eternity of Israel manifests. This is particularly relevant to the blessing of the month of Sivan, when Rebbe Ze'ev Wolf wrote his letter to Rebbe Menachem Mendel. It is then that we merit the 50th Gate of Understanding, which is expanded consciousness.

Rabbi Shalom of Kaminka:
Peeling Potatoes was Never so Lofty

Rabbi Shalom Rosenfeld, the rabbi of Kaminka and the founding father of the Kaminka dynasty, was born to the philanthropist Yaakov Yosef, and Yenta, the daughter of Rabbi Yehoshua Tzvi Heschel of Behr. He finished the entire Talmud at the age of 9. In his youth, he studied under the tutelage of Rabbi Tzvi Hirsch Harif and Rabbi Shlomo Kluger and later became a *chassid* and disciple of Rebbe Naftoli of Ropschitz. Rabbi Shalom, who never officially served as a chassidic rebbe, was known as a great and brilliant *tzaddik*. Many of his teachings are intertwined with witticisms that conceal supernal secrets. He passed away on the 20th of Cheshvan, 5612 (1851). His only son, Rabbi Yehoshua, succeeded him in Kaminka. His Torah teachings and stories about him were printed in the book, *'Ohev Shalom.'*

After the passing of his rebbe and teacher, Rabbi Naftoli of Ropschitz, Rabbi Shalom of Kaminka learned under the tutelage of Rabbi Sar Shalom of Belz. Once Rabbi Sar Shalom told Rabbi Shalom to prepare himself well to study a special unification for the time when a soul is departing this world. When he exited Rabbi Sar Shalom's room after learning the unification, Rabbi Shalom was confronted by Rabbi Sar Shalom's famously righteous wife, Malkah. "Did you ever learn such amazing revelations with your previous Rebbe?" she asked. Rebbe Shalom attempted to avoid answering her, but ultimately replied:

"Once I was sitting in the kitchen in Ropschitz with Rabbi Chaim of Sanz, peeling potatoes for everyone's meal. Suddenly, the holy Rebbe Naftali entered, put his hand on my shoulder and his other hand on Rebbe Chaim's shoulder and taught us the unification for peeling potatoes. This is the same unification that I now learned from Rabbi Sar Shalom."

What does the departure of the soul from the body have to do with peeling potatoes? We can imagine that the number of potatoes that needed to be peeled in Ropschitz was enough to make anyone's soul depart from their body, but that is not the only connection…

The departure of the soul from the body is the separation of the internal soul from the external body. This can be compared to separating the fruit from its peel. This is the secret of the verse (from which this unification is learned), "And you will go to your fathers in peace, you will be buried at a good old age,"[1] which God said to Abraham. "And you will go to your fathers in peace" refers to the soul-fruit, which departs from the body, while "you will be buried at a good old age" refers to the burial of the body-peel. The numerical value of this entire verse equals "good" 22 (טוֹבָה) times "pleasure" 123 (עֹנֶג), alluding to "good pleasure." "Good" (טוֹבָה) is also the final word in this verse.

Another story about the two friends, Rabbi Shalom of Kaminka and Rabbi Chaim of Sanz in the Ropschitz kitchen:

Once, Rabbi Shalom and Rabbi Chaim were peeling potatoes in Rebbe Naftali of Ropschitz's kitchen.

Suddenly, the Rebbe entered the kitchen and vigorously threw a potato into the water-filled pot there. Water splashed everywhere and Rabbi Naftali said to them, "And I will throw upon you pure waters and you will be purified."[1] From that time on, a spirit of purity dwelled upon them.

Since the destruction of the Holy Temple in Jerusalem, we lack the purification of the purifying waters prepared with the ashes of the red heifer). Only in the future will the verse that the Ropschitzer Rebbe said be fulfilled. But for true *tzaddikim*, even a potato, which in Hebrew is called a *tapu'ach* **adamah** can serve the purpose of a *parah* **adumah** (red heifer; in Hebrew, **adumah** is cognate to **adamah**)—and can transform kitchen work to service in the Holy Temple in purity.

---

1.   Ezekiel 36:25.

Rebbe Tzvi Hirsch of Rimanov: A Guide to Keeping Heaven Happy:

Rebbe Tzvi Hirsch Hakohen of Rimanov was the student and successor of Rebbe Menachem Mendel of Rimanov. Rebbe Tzvi Hirsch was orphaned at a young age and when he came to the study hall of Rabbi Menachem Mendel of Rimanov, the *chassidim* there felt sorry for him and learned Torah with him. Eventually, Rebbe Tzvi Hirsch became Rebbe Mendele's personal assistant, and he became known as Rebbe Tzvi Hirsch the Assistant. Rebbe Menachem Mendele instructed that Rebbe Tzvi Hirsch should succeed him, and after his passing, Rebbe Tzvi Hirsch became the leader of the Rimanov chassidic congregation and many other *chassidim*, including the *tzaddikim* of that generation, would travel to see him. Rebbe Tzvi Hirsch passed away on the 30th of Cheshvan 5607 (1846). He is buried in Rimanov, Galicia, which today is in Poland.

When Rebbe Tzvi Hirsch was a young boy, his parents passed away and little Tzvi Hirsch was sent to learn a trade with a tailor. Even at that young age, the boy's heart burned with desire to serve God, to be connected to *tzaddikim,* and to lead his life according to the teachings of the Ba'al Shem Tov. After a short time with the tailor, young Tzvi Hirsch ran away and came to the study hall of Rebbe Menachem Mendel of Rimanov, where he began his life as a devoted follower and *chassid.*

As a child, Rebbe Tzvi Hirsch would pray with intense devotion and concentration. Even after he matured and became Rebbe Mendele's personal assistant, he continued to pray with intensity. Often, when his ardent fervor would overflow, Rebbe Tzvi Hirsch would run from end to end of the synagogue, still completely focused on his prayer. If he would run into someone or something while running in this state of divestment from the physical, he would simply pick him or it up and continue running with fervor and devotion to God, unaware of the additional passenger in his arms.

Once on *Rosh Chodesh* (the first day of the Hebrew month), a wealthy man came to see Rebbe Mendele. As is the way with the wealthy, this man was dressed in fine, expensive clothing. He did not know Rebbe Tzvi Hirsch and was not prepared for what happened next. When the man entered Rebbe Mendele's study hall, Rebbe Tzvi Hirsch was running from end to end with his intense devotion. Suddenly, he ran into the man, and without missing a beat—as he was in a state of divestment from the physical—Rebbe Tzvi Hirsch picked him up and proceeded to run with him from end to end. Not only that, but while he was running, the edge of the man's fine coat was torn. The flabbergasted man was quite beside himself. But he saw that Rebbe Tzvi Hirsch looked very righteous and thinking that perhaps he was Rebbe Mendele's son, decided not to make a fuss about it.

After the prayer service, the *chassidim* sat down to the festive *Rosh Chodesh* meal. The wealthy man saw that

Rebbe Mendele called Rebbe Tzvi Hirsch to serve the food and understood that the young man who had torn his coat was simply the Rebbe's assistant and not his son. The man became angry and indignantly turned to the Rebbe, "What is going on here? Your assistant is a damage-causing ox! The Rebbe keeps an ox who rams into people here!" The man continued to tell the Rebbe how his assistant had run with him in his arms during prayers and how he had torn his coat. "And why don't you reprimand him?" the man demanded of the Rebbe.

Similar to stories of the Alter Rebbe and other *tzaddikim*, Rebbe Mendele entered a state of devotion to God, leaned on the table with his head in his hand, and stayed that way for quite some time. Eventually, the Rebbe raised his head, turned to the man, and said to him, "In Heaven, they are not angry at Rebbe Tzvi Hirsch, and *I* should be angry at him? Even though he was over-energetic and even caused you some damage and tore your coat, I cannot reprimand him and tell him to stop, because in Heaven, they are not angry with him. On the contrary, it seems that his fervent prayer generates great joy in Heaven. And you want *me* to be angry at him?"

Whoever Does Not Resort to Anger
does not Provoke Anger

We can learn many things from this story. First of all, we see that Rebbe Tzvi Hirsch prayed with complete seriousness. He was not fooling around or acting wildly. He was simply serving

God with devotion. Rebbe Mendele said that in Heaven, they were not angry with Rebbe Tzvi Hirsch. This teaches us a major principle in Chassidut: Whatever we do here on earth, takes place in Heaven Above, as well. To use the idiom of the *Zohar* (1:88a), "An awakening from below engenders an awakening Above."[1] Heaven conducts itself toward you in the manner that you conduct yourself here on earth. If in Heaven they were not angry with Rebbe Tzvi Hirsch the reason apparently was that he himself did not ever become angry with anyone here on earth. And in fact, Rebbe Tzvi Hirsch testified about himself at the end of his life that, "All my days, I did not become angry and never felt acrimony toward anyone." The fact that a person never becomes angry and does not feel acrimony toward others frees him to serve God with utmost devotion, like a freed prisoner. Then, even if he runs into somebody and they do not understand what is happening, in Heaven they are happy with him, smiling and laughing together with him. Even if someone does feel acrimonious toward him, like the wealthy man in our story, Heaven determines that they are not displeased and thus, there is no reason to be displeased here on earth.

Even a Simple Boy can become a Rebbe

There is another very important lesson that we can learn from Rebbe Tzvi Hirsch. Rebbe Tzvi Hirsch was a simple boy who came from a simple family. His father was a tailor and he started out as the assistant of Rebbe Mendele of Raminov. How did that happen? One time, the young Tzvi Hirsch had the merit to make up Rebbe Mendele's bed. Rebbe Mendele, with his holy, inner understanding, realized that there was something very

---

1.   See also *Tanya* c. 27 and *Or hachaim* to Exodus 19:3.

special about Tzvi Hirsch and from that point on, he became the personal assistant of the great Rebbe.

When Rebbe Mendele passed away, he gave instructions that his successor would not be one of his sons or one of his great disciples, but rather, his assistant, Rebbe Tzvi Hirsch. Even the simplest Jew from the simplest background can be a Rebbe.

The Lubavitcher Rebbe taught that in our generation, everyone has to be a Rebbe. What is a Rebbe? Someone who takes responsibility upon himself to bring another Jew closer to God.

Rebbe Tzvi Hirsch of Rimanov: Sensing God's Will

A widow lived in Rimanov with her six children. For months, she couldn't pay her rent. The landlord wanted to evict her, but being a *chassid*, he went to ask the town rabbi what to do. The rabbi determined that according to Torah law, he could evict her. The landlord informed the widow that if she would not pay by a certain date, she would be evicted from her home.

The widow came to Rebbe Tzvi Hirsch of Rimanov in tears. "Who said this?" asked the Rebbe. "The landlord," she answered, according to the decision of the town rabbi." Without thinking twice, Rebbe Tzvi Hirsch rose and went to the rabbi to clarify the matter. "That is what is written in the *Choshen Mishpat!*" the town rabbi claimed. "It is a clear law!"

"I honor you very much, but I would like to see the law myself," Rebbe Tzvi Hirsch answered. "Can you please open the book for me in the right place so that I may read it?"

The rabbi opened the book, looked, clutched his head and looked again. "It is just the opposite! I made a mistake," the rabbi said in dismay. "It says that in this type of case, it is prohibited to evict the tenant!"

"How did you know?" the Rebbe's students asked him. "I didn't know," Rebbe Tzvi Hirsch answered. "I am not an expert in the financial law. But when this woman came in, I felt such great compassion for her, that my heart told me that it cannot be that in the Torah of God, the Merciful Father, there could be such a cruel ruling."

Once Rebbe Zusha of Anapoli found the solution for a complicated problem in Jewish law. Later, this solution was discovered in the Jerusalem Talmud, Rebbe Zusha explained, "I am not familiar with the Jerusalem Talmud. But I perceived the solution from the same place that the Jerusalem Talmud perceived it."

The story about Rebbe Tzvi Hirsch is different than the story about Rebbe Zusha. Knowing himself and his Creator, Rebbe Tzvi Hirsch was sure that his feelings were in line with God's will. Not only was his heart tuned in to the Divine wavelength, but his body could also feel holiness and was drawn to it, as the following story will illustrate:

Everyone knew Rebbe Tzvi Hirsch as the Rebbe's assistant, an orphan boy whose lineage was not illustrious. When he became a Rebbe, there were still those who held him in disdain. Once, Rebbe Tzvi Hirsch went to visit the *Yeshuot Yaakov*, who was one of the greatest scholars of Jewish law in the world in that era. With complete disdain for Rebbe Tzvi Hirsch, the *Yeshuot Yaakov* told his family to remove all the chairs from the house so that Rebbe Tzvi Hirsch would not be able to sit down.

Rebbe Tzvi Hirsch arrived and put his hand on the mezuzah to kiss it. But his hand remained on the mezuzah, as if it was glued there. He could not remove his hand from the mezuzah in order to kiss it, as is customary. "Are you implying that my mezuzah is not kosher?" the *Yeshuot Yaakov* said to him with contempt. I just checked it a few weeks ago, and it is absolutely kosher!" They called in the most expert scribe in the city, but even before he arrived, they removed the mezuzah from the doorpost and saw that the person who had re-hung the mezuzah after it had been checked had punctured it with the nail that affixed it to the doorpost. There was no question at all. Clearly, the mezuzah was completely unkosher.

The *Yeshuot Yaakov* immediately called for chairs to be brought in, and his entire approach to Rebbe Tzvi Hirsch became respectful.

"How did you know that the mezuzah was unkosher?" he asked. "I didn't know," answered Rebbe Tzvi Hirsch. "But when I raise my hand to the mezuzah and I feel a good feeling (today we would call it 'positive energy') then I know that the mezuzah is fine. And if not…"

The *chassidim* who were present said that the greatest wonder of all was that they saw no change in Rebbe Tzvi Hirsch throughout his meeting with the Yeshuot Yaakov between the time that the Yeshuot Yaakov treated him with contempt and the time that he afforded him great honor.

How did Rebbe Tzvi Hirsch acquire this sense? We can discern the answer from the words of a different *tzaddik,* Rebbe Yisrael of Ruzhin. He said that there is nothing novel about him being a *tzaddik:* his father, grandfather and great-grandfather were all *tzaddikim.* But Rebbe Tzvi Hirsch the Assistant is a novel phenomenon: "He took rough leather and turned it into delicate silk."

In Chabad, the word for 'work' (*avodah*) is cognate to the word for 'refinement' (*ibud*). We must refine our character in the same manner that leather is refined. This is the ultimate purpose of our service of God. Those who merit to attain it feel holiness throughout their bodies and emotions. This is the gentle, ephemeral element that hovers above reality.

> When the Rebbe of Ruzhin and Rebbe Tzvi Hirsch became in-laws, the Ruzhiner, as was his custom, recounted his lineage "The Maggid of Mezritch, Rebbe Abraham the Angel, and his father, Rebbe Shalom of Parhovitch. When he finished recounting his lineage, he turned to Rebbe Tzvi Hirsch and said, "Now it is *your* turn to recount *your* lineage." "My father was a simple tailor," Rebbe Tzvi Hirsch answered. "I remember one thing that he taught me: An old article of clothing should be mended, and take care not to ruin a new article of clothing."
>
> "That is quite sufficient," the Rebbe of Ruzhin replied.

THE MITTLER REBBE: SEARCHING FOR THE EVIL WITHIN

Rebbe Dov Ber Schneori, the Mittler Rebbe, is the second Rebbe in the Chabad dynasty. He was the son and successor of the Alter Rebbe of Chabad, Rabbi Schneor Zalman of Liadi. The Mittler Rebbe was born after the passing of the Maggid of Mezritch and was named after him. He is known for the length and depth of his chassidic discourses–so much so that his son-in-law, the third Rebbe, the *Tzemach Tzedek* said that "If they would cut my father-in-law's finger, blood would not spurt out, but rather, chassidic teachings." Like his father, the Mittler Rebbe was also imprisoned because of the accusations of those opposed to Chassidut. His day of redemption from prison is the tenth of Kislev. The day before that, the ninth of Kislev is his birthday and day of passing. Being born and passing away on the same date is an expression of the verse, "I shall fill the number of your days."

The Mittler Rebbe was the head of Chabad for 15 years. He died while writing a chassidic discourse and is buried in Nizhyn, Ukraine.

On one of the Mittler Rebbe's journeys, a young Torah scholar entered his chamber for a private audience (called a *yechidut*). Following this discussion, the Rebbe locked himself in his room in the inn and did not eat nor drink nor receive anyone else for private meetings. The *chassidim* were very surprised by the Rebbe's unusual conduct. Those who managed to peek inside the Rebbe's chambers saw an awesome sight: The Rebbe was sitting in his room and reciting Psalms, while his eyes shed tears ceaselessly. Nobody knew why.

After three days, the Rebbe announced that he would renew consultation hours. He ate, became stronger and just a few days later, set out for the rest of his journey.

The senior *chassidim* with the Rebbe waited for an opportunity to speak to him directly and questioned him about his unusual behavior.

The Mittler Rebbe related: "On that day, a young Torah student confessed a sin to me and asked how he could rectify his situation. You know that a Rebbe cannot advise a rectification for someone else's sin if he cannot find a trace of the same sin within himself, albeit in a practically intangible spiritual manner, not in action, as has been performed by the person seeking his help. He must find some spiritual fault that corresponds to the sin in the most subtle manner. What the young man told me left me shaken, and no matter how much I searched inside me, I did not find a trace of that sin. Then I realized that the sin that he related to me is completely in my unconscious. I am totally unaware of it. It is an aspect of the evil world inside me. I have evil inside me and I am not conscious of it. That is something that requires repentance, and that is what I did. After three days of fasting, repentance and reciting Psalms, I found the trace of the sin within myself. It was only then that I could advise the young man on how to rectify his negative actions."

The Mittler Rebbe fasted, repented and recited Psalms with tears for three days until he discovered the hidden evil, a trace of a trace—in his soul. If a person has evil within him, he must be aware of it. By being conscious of our hidden evil, we can rectify it in ourselves and then find the correct rectification for others. This is in keeping with how the Ba'al Shem Tov explained the verse, "Rebuke, rebuke your colleague,"[1]—First rebuke yourself, and afterward, you will be able to rebuke your colleague.

As long as we have hidden evil in our souls, we are not at the level of the *tzaddik*. The *tzaddik* is in control of his unconscious. The intermediate person, on the other hand, is in control only of his consciousness: thought, speech and action. He does not have access to his unconscious and certainly has no control over it. If the Mittler Rebbe could not find within himself a trace of a trace of something that is abstractly similar to the sin related to him, it is a sign that he too still had hidden evil of which he was not conscious. For this, a *tzaddik* of his stature must do *teshuvah* with great self-sacrifice.

In addition, as long as the *tzaddik* has some hidden evil within him, he can make mistakes in judgment. Mistaken judgment is most highly improbable for a *tzaddik*, but such a reality does exist. One of the tasks of the Mashiach is to rectify the hidden evil in the soul. There will be no more hidden evil and the verse, "And the spirit of impurity, I will remove from the land,"[2] will be fulfilled. When we reach that destiny, there will no longer be any possibility of mistaken judgment.

---

1. Leviticus 19:17.
2. Zechariah 13:2.

THE MAGGID OF MEZRITCH:
SELF-NULLIFICATION ON THE PRECIPICE

Rabbi Dov Ber of Mezritch, known as the Maggid of Mezritch, was the greatest disciple of the Ba'al Shem Tov. He was born in Lukatch, Ukraine. His father, Rabbi Avraham, was descended from the Mishnaic sage, Rabbi Yochanan Hasandlar, and generations before, from King David. As a child, Rabbi Dov Ber was obviously brilliant and his father sent him to study Torah in the yeshivah of the *Pnei Yehoshua* (Rabbi Yaakov Yehosuha Falk) in Levov. After his marriage, he was a teacher in Toltshin and began learning Kabbalah. Later, he was a maggid (a preacher) in a number of villages.

As soon as Rabbi Dov Ber came to the Ba'al Shem Tov, he became his principle disciple. After the Ba'al She Tov's passing, his son, Rabbi Tzvi, was appointed to lead the Ba'al Shem Tov's disciples. A year later, during the festive Shavu'ot meal on the first anniversary of the Ba'al Shem Tov's passing, Rabbi Tzvi announced that his father had appeared to him and instructed him to transfer the leadership position to Rabbi Dov Ber. Rabbi Tzvi rose from his place and gave the Maggid his topcoat, which had belonged to the Ba'al Shem Tov, and then the Maggid sat in Rabbi Tzvi's place and began to teach Torah.

Unlike his Rabbi, the Ba'al Shem Tov, who would travel from place to place, the Maggid stayed in Mezritch and from there sent his students to teach Torah and establish centers of chassidic life throughout Russia, Poland and even Germany. A few months before he passed away, the Maggid moved to Anapoli due to a plague that had broken out in Mezritch. He passed away on 19 Kislev 5633 (1872) and is buried in Anapoli.

The great chassidic *aliyah* to the Land of Israel came from the

Maggid's study hall, led by his disciple, Rabbi Menachem Mendel of Vitebsk who made *aliyah* in 1777. Among the Maggid's other famous disciples were his son, Rabbi Avraham the Angel, the Alter Rebbe of Chabad, the brothers, Rabbi Zusha of Anapoli and Rabbi Elimelech of Lizhensk, Rabbi Aharon the Great of Karlin, the brothers Rabbi Pinchas Ba'al Hahafla'ah and Rabbi Shmelkeh of Nikolsburg, Rabbi Yehudah Leib Hakohen, Rabbi Ze'ev of Zhitomer and many more.

Our story about the Maggid begins when the holy brothers, Rabbi Shmelkeh and Rabbi Pinchas first came to the Maggid. They wanted to ask him to guide them—to prescribe them a path for serving of God.

"Why did you travel to me? After all, you lack nothing. You are great in Torah, both revealed and concealed and you serve God. You do not need me," said the Maggid as soon as he saw them.

"Nonetheless," the brothers answered, we came to ask you to guide us in our service of God."

"When you rise for the Midnight Prayer," the Maggid answered, "first wash your hands ritually, with all the intentions of the holy Ari. After that, say the morning blessings, recite the Midnight prayer with all the intentions, study Torah with true cleaving to God until the morning light. Afterward, immerse in the *mikveh* with all the intentions of the Ari, pray the Morning Prayer with cleaving to God, for a very long time. And if after all of that, one of you may think that "I just gave my Creator pleasure," God will take all that you did from the moment that you rose at midnight, will make a ball out of all your service and will throw it into the mouth of the deep abyss."

"Really, we should not have traveled by wagon to you," said the brothers. "We should have crawled here on all fours, the entire way!"

The final statement spoken by the holy brothers demonstrates the quintessence of self-nullification (when it is unified with lowliness). It is the feeling that all of my accomplishments are condensed into a tiny point (symbolizing the *sefirah* of kingdom) and thrown into the mouth of the so-called great abyss, the *sefirah* of kingdom of the *sitra achra* (the other side).

Let us explain. The founders of Chassidut, the Ba'al Shem Tov, the Maggid, and the Alter Rebbe had identified two attributes that are the essence of Divine service: cleaving to God (דְּבֵקוּת) and self-nullification (בִּטּוּל). Cleaving to God is the light (by cleaving we reveal the Divine—all revelation is called "light"). self-nullification provides the vessel, the state of the rectified vessel that can contain the light of cleaving. Both cleaving and Self-nullification—both the light and the vessel—are essential for prayer.

Even though hatred of the self that feels separate from God started with the Ba'al Shem Tov (thus requiring self-nullification, the nullification of the separate self), in the Ba'al Shem Tov's teaching we find that the stress is on cleaving to God, while self-nullification is implied as already included in the cleaving. Thus, the vessel was included in the light. This is an example of the Kabbalistic principle that, "from the thickening of the light, the vessels came into being" (מֵהִתְעַבּוּת הָאוֹרוֹת נִתְהַוּוּ הַכֵּלִים). When the Ba'al Shem Tov and his disciples prayed, the main aspect was their cleaving to God. The self-nullification was also there, but it was concealed.

The Maggid's novel path was to separate the self-nullification from the cleaving to God, to speak about the vessel—self-nullification—and its rectification. He separated self-nullification from the cleaving and set it as a separate and distinct pillar of service of God. Thus, in the Maggid's teachings, there were already two distinct pillars of Divine service: the pillar of cleaving to God and the pillar of self-nullification.

[After the Maggid's passing, each of his holy disciples took a different aspect of his teachings. For instance, Rebbe Levi Yitzchak of Berditchev took the pillar of clinging to God during prayer. When people saw him pray, they would see the greatness of the light he revealed—it was like watching a lightning storm. The Alter Rebbe, Rabbi Shneur Zalman of Liadi, who founded Chabad, begged his companions to increase the vessels—to make many vessels that would spread the light that Chassidut had accessed and brought down into the world. To create vessels, one has to focus on self-nullification. Thus, in Chabad teachings, one hardly hears about the pillar of cleaving to God. It is not missing, simply concealed in a lengthy process described, for example, in Rebbe Hillel of Paritch's commentary on the Mittler Rebbe's *Sha'ar Hayichud*. In any case, the Alter Rebbe reversed the situation from the Ba'al Shem Tov's stress on cleaving to God with self-nullification included therein to a state in which the stress is on self-nullification and cleaving to God.]

But, since the brothers were Torah giants, their first meeting with the Maggid did not end with that. The story continues:

> The brothers asked the Maggid to honor them by discussing some of the revealed aspects of the Torah. The Maggid began elucidating a very complex topic in Torah and then proceeded to reveal grave difficulties with his own explanation. He then responded to these difficulties himself, with genius. After he had

laid all the difficulties to rest, he revealed another major flaw with his rebuttal, which essentially contradicted its entire reasoning. He then responded to the original difficulties in a different manner, building an entire construct of intricate Torah detail. And then he again razed the construct to the ground. The Maggid repeated this nine times. His power of complex reasoning was so honed and deep, that the two Torah geniuses had to squeeze their heads in order to employ every ounce of their intellect just to follow it.

After the brothers left, the Maggid remarked that they "almost pushed me down."

* * *

What did the Maggid mean with this last statement?

We can learn the answer from something similar that the Ba'al Shem Tov once said. The Ba'al Shem Tov's grandson, Rabbi Moshe Chaim of Sudilkov (later known as the *Degel Machaneh Efraim* after his book) relates that once, when he was a little boy, he was sitting on his grandfather's lap and the Ba'al Shem Tov said to him, "Believe me that there is in every generation one individual who hears Torah—not from the mouth of an angel and not from the mouth of a *saraf* (fiery angel), but rather from the mouth of the Almighty and His Divine Presence. Yet this individual is in constant fear of falling into the great abyss if for one second he will think highly of himself." This is also connected to what the Ba'al Shem Tov said moments before he passed away (Psalms 36:12), "Let not the foot of pride overtake me," (אַל תְּבוֹאֵנִי רֶגֶל גַּאֲוָה), something that is also told about the holy Arizal.

What the Maggid was saying was that in order to speak such great Torah learning as he had before the two brothers, he had to knowingly put himself in danger of becoming aware of his own greatness. But, because of his love of his fellow Jews, because of his concern that the two brothers attach to the light of Chassidut through himself, he had brought himself to the very precipice of the great abyss, teetering on the very edge of losing his self-nullification. However, in the end he was successful in preventing his fall.

The Alter Rebbe, the Jailer and the New Moon

The Alter Rebbe (18 Elul 5505 [1745]–24 Tevet 5573 [1812] was the founder of the Chassidut of Chabad and the author of the *Shulchan Aruch Harav* and the seminal chassidic work, the *Tanya*.

Just a short time after the Alter Rebbe was jailed in a Russian prison on false charges of treason, his Russian prison guard realized that the Jew under his watch was a holy man of God. When the Alter Rebbe asked his jailer to allow him to leave the dungeon in order to say the *Kiddush Levana* prayer on the new moon at its proper time, the jailer hesitated. If he would be caught allowing a prisoner to emerge from the dungeon against the rules, he would be killed. After some negotiation, however, the jailer agreed to allow the Alter Rebbe to pray outside as he requested, under one condition: "Give me a written guarantee that I will live a long life of wealth and honor in this world, and I will allow you to go outside," he said to the Alter Rebbe. And the Alter Rebbe actually did write out a promise for a long life of wealth and honor in this world and gave it to the jailer.

A promise for long life is no simple matter—even for a *tzaddik* like the Ba'al Shem Tov. It requires a dimension of self-sacrifice. Nonetheless, the Alter Rebbe was willing to make this self-sacrifice in order to pray the *Kiddush Levana* prayer outside at the right time.

After receiving his guarantee, the jailer led the Alter Rebbe outside to an uncovered courtyard from where he would be able to see the moon. "It is now eleven-thirty," he said to the Rebbe. "At midnight the new guard comes on duty. You must be back inside by then. If the new guard realizes that I allowed you outside, I will be in danger and you will certainly be in even more danger." The Alter Rebbe began to say the *Kiddush Levana* prayer with enthusiasm. Half an hour went by and he did not finish. His prayer went on and on. But the new guard did not show up. When the Alter Rebbe completed his prayer, more than an hour had passed. The jailer was livid but could do nothing. At the second that the jailer locked the Alter Rebbe into his cell, the new guard arrived.

The new guard, who was over an hour late, knew that if the first guard would report him, he would be in trouble. He fell at his feet, begging him not to report him, and explained: "I don't understand what happened to me. For twenty years, I have been taking the same route from my home to the prison every night. I have never lost my way. Tonight, when I left my home, I didn't know the way. I began walking from one place to the next, getting more and more confused. Only now, after over an hour—I finally found my way." The first jailer, understanding that a miracle had just taken place, promised not to report his tardy replacement.

How did this miraculous story become known?

Forty or fifty years later, some of the *chassidim* of the third Lubavitcher Rebbe, the *Tzemach Tzedek,* were researching the imprisonment of the Alter Rebbe. They went to the archives of the prison where the Alter Rebbe had been jailed and bribed the clerk there to open the archive for them. They wanted to uncover every detail of the Alter Rebbe's imprisonment. "Wait a bit," said the clerk. "Soon the general responsible for the archives will come here to perform a short check of the archives. He only comes once a month and then you will have a full month to dig deep into the archives and find what you are looking for."

The *chassidim* waited and sure enough, the general came, performed a perfunctory check of the archives and left. The clerk opened the archive and the *chassidim* began turning piles of papers over, searching for documents about the Alter Rebbe. Suddenly, the door opened again and in walked the general. He had forgotten something in the archive and came to retrieve it. The *chassidim* were caught red-handed. They didn't know what to do and simply fell at the general's feet. "We did not come to do anything against the law," they begged. "We are Chabad *chassidim.* Two generations ago, our Rebbe was imprisoned here and we are searching for information about what happened during his imprisonment."

Much to their amazement, the general's face lit up, and instead of having them dragged off to prison, he invited them to his private room, where he began his story. "I was the jailer of your first Rebbe," he told the flabbergasted group of *chassidim*, relating what happened that night of *Kiddush Levanah*. "Your Rebbe's promise to me was completely fulfilled. I am an old man, a general and I enjoy wealth and respect". The general removed the Alter Rebbe's handwritten guarantee from his drawer, showed it to the *chassidim* and related how it was fulfilled:

"I was a simple jailer, and after some time, I was transferred to guard duty at the gates of the prison. One day, as I was standing at the gate, the carriage of the Czar himself came by. Inside the carriage were the Czar and his family. Suddenly, the door of the carriage opened and one of the Czar's sons was about to fall out. I ran and caught the child, saving him from serious injury and possible death. The carriage stopped, the Czar exited and asked me,

'Are you the guard here at the gate?'

'Yes', I answered.

'Do you know that you deserve the death penalty for leaving your post?' he said.

'Even though I deserve the death penalty,' I answered, 'I am willing to die in order to save the son of the Czar.'

When the Czar heard my answer, he said to me, 'If so, I will make you a general. That is a fitting reward for someone who performs such a deed'.

"The problem was that I had no military training", the general continued, "so the Czar made me an honorary general and gave me a job that does not require military knowledge. I am the general of the archive and have lived a very long life of wealth and honor," he concluded.

* * *

Kiddush Levana is a special *mitzvah*. The sages call this *mitzvah*, "*Kabbalat panim*" — a reception — for our Father in Heaven. What is so special about this *mitzvah*? It is a messianic *mitzvah*, heralding the revelation of the Mashiach with the words, "*David melech Yisrael chai v'kayam*" ("David, the King of Israel lives and exists"). The Jewish people are likened to the moon, bases its calendar according to the moon and thus, in the future, will be renewed like the moon.

From the first part of this story, we see how dear the *mitzvah* of *Kiddush Levana* was to the Alter Rebbe. In our times, the Lubavitcher Rebbe encouraged everyone — including women — to perform this *mitzvah*. Who was at work behind the scenes of this story, causing the guard to be posted at the gate and having the Czar's son fall? The Alter Rebbe. But there is a deeper dimension here. The Alter Rebbe imbued his jailer with a pinch of his own self-sacrifice, which gave him the idea to tell the Czar that he was willing to sacrifice his life for his son. It all began with the Alter Rebbe's devotion to Torah and *mitzvot* in general, and particularly to the *mitzvah* of *Kiddush Levana* — permeating all the space and people surrounding him with a bit of his own self-sacrifice.

The Alter Rebbe: God's Inestimable Pleasure When You Don't Sin

The Ba'al Shem Tov said about himself that he came to the world in order to infuse the service of repentance with vitality. Until the time of the Ba'al Shem Tov, repentance *(teshuvah)* was dreaded as a dreary process replete with sadness, fasting and harshness. The innovative teaching of Chassidut is that our constant service of *teshuvah* should be done with vitality and joy for the opportunity that we have to come close to God. In the following story, the Alter Rebbe of Chabad and author of the *Tanya*, Rabbi Shneur Zalman of Liadi, teaches us how precious *teshuvah* is to God—even if it is incomplete.

In every chassidic community, there was a special charity called *maamad gelt*, charity given for the Rebbe himself. This money was used to support the Rebbe and his household, and it was considered a special privilege to donate for that purpose. Every year, all the *chassidim* in the community would give their *maamad gelt* to one of the elders of the community. The elder would travel to the Rebbe, bringing him a list of all the donors and their families, with the amount that they had contributed.

One year, one of the elders came to the Alter Rebbe with his list of donors. The Rebbe, who remembered everything, looked at the list and saw that one of the donors was missing. The Alter Rebbe had tens of thousands of *chassidim,* but remembered each and every one of them and saw that somebody was missing. "What happened to him?" he asked.

The elder *chassid* sheepishly told the Rebbe, that the person in question had unfortunately left the chassidic lifestyle, and even worse, had left the Jewish lifestyle altogether. "After this Jew left the fold, we distanced him from our prayer quorum," the elder continued. "He no longer prays with us and so we were not able to request his annual donation."

The Alter Rebbe became very serious, and said to him, "You cannot estimate what being in the close vicinity of a chassidic *shtiebel* (synagogue) does for the soul. And you cannot estimate how much pleasure there is Above when a Jew does one less sin."

* * *

The Alter Rebbe did not tell the veteran *chassid* to make sure that wayward Jew would do *teshuvah.* Instead, he said that it was not right to distance him, for although he had left the fold and was sinning, if he would still remain in the community, perhaps he would do one less sin. And we cannot even imagine how much pleasure God has when a Jew does one less sin.

The Alter Rebbe taught us a way of doing *teshuvah* that is not explicitly *teshuva.* When the *chassidim* distanced the wayward Jew, they were motivated by the outer dimension of the *sefirah* of understanding (*binah*), from where harsh judgment awakens. But the Alter Rebbe's statement, that you cannot begin to estimate the great pleasure Above when a Jew does one less sin, stems from the inner dimension of the persona called "Mother" (*Imma*), where severe judgments are sweetened at their source. Thus, instead of distancing this Jew, he should be drawn near.

In his *Igeret Hateshuvah* in the *Tanya*, we understand from the Alter Rebbe that a person who is considered a master of repentance (*ba'al teshuvah*) is someone who will never re-commit the sin in question. If not, according to the *Igeret Hateshuvah*, it is not really repentance The Alter Rebbe's son, the Mittler Rebbe, wrote in *Derech Chaim* that if a Jew strives to do complete *teshuva* but does not exactly succeed—he suffers from constant setbacks and failure—he should remember the verses "A *tzaddik* falls seven times and rises[1]," "And Your Nation are all *tzaddikim*[2]," and "Although I have fallen I have arisen[3]." The very effort brings great pleasure to God.

According to the plain meaning of the *Tanya* and according to the Rambam's Laws of *Teshuvah*, a person who does *teshuva* and then falls back into the same sin has not really done *teshuva*. We cannot testify to the fact that he will no longer commit this sin, as the Rambam prescribes as a measure of his success, because he has setbacks and failures. But the Mittler Rebbe says that despite his failures, his effort brings great pleasure to God.

The idea in our story is even more powerful than what the Mittler Rebbe wrote. This story is about a Jew who is not interested in doing *teshuvah* (at least not consciously). But when the *chassidim* continue to invite him to their community events, such as a *farbrengen*, and during the time that he is with them,

---

1.　Proverbs 24:16.
2.　Isaiah 60:21.
3.　Micah 7:8.

he does one less sin than he would have done if he had not been with them, we cannot begin to estimate the great pleasure that this causes in Heaven.

If so, our story discusses three levels of the inner dimension of *Imma*, where the secret of *teshuvah* resides:

- The simple meaning of *teshuvah*, in which the person does not commit the sin ever again.
- The *teshuva* explained by the Mittler Rebbe—that a person attempts to repent, but fails, gets back up and tries again. And fails.
- The *teshuva* that the Alter Rebbe teaches here—that even one sin less brings inestimable pleasure on High.

Rebbe Zusha Stories for Sukkot

Rabbi Meshulam Zusil of Anapoli, better known as Rebbe Zusha, was a senior student of the Maggid of Mezritch. Brother of the renowned Rebbe Elimelech of Lizhansk, Rebbe Zusha is known to have been a Torah scholar and a genius in earnestness and sincerity. Many of the stories about him highlight his earnest nature. He passed away on 2 Shevat, 5560 (1800) and was brought to rest in the gravesite of the Rav the Maggid of Anapoli.

Object of a *Mitzvah*

For many years, Rebbe Zusha wandered through Jewish towns in "exile." Once, on one of his journeys, his clothing became particularly tattered. When he came to a Jewish town, most of the people were put off by his appearance and did not want to invite him into their homes. With no other choice, the synagogue beadle invited Rebbe Zusha to his home. While Rebbe Zusha was eating the modest meal that the beadle set before him, he began to kiss his own hands. The beadle thought that perhaps his guest was not only poor, but also deranged. Nonetheless, he asked him why he was kissing his hands.

"There is a fruit called an *etrog*," Rebbe Zusha answered. "All year long, it is just a fruit like all other fruits. But when Sukkot comes, it becomes a tool for doing a *mitzvah*, and then this fruit becomes extremely important. The same goes for me. I am really nothing. But now I have had the merit that a fellow Jew was able to fulfill the great *mitzvah* of hosting guests through me. My body is like an *etrog*. So just like we love the *etrog* so much that we kiss it, I am kissing myself because my body has become a vehicle for a *mitzvah*...

Keep Calm

Rebbe Zusha had very exceptional and valuable *tefillin*. Once, before Sukkot, he didn't have any money at all to buy the four species. Rebbe Zusha sold his *tefillin* and bought an exceptional *etrog* with the money.

When his wife found out, she was extremely upset. She knew how valuable the *tefillin* were and could not understand how Rebbe Zusha could sell them for a *mitzvah* that lasts one week only. In her fury, she took the *etrog* and bit off its end, rendering it ritually useless. Rebbe Zusha saw what happened and did not react. Afterward, Heaven revealed to him that his silence after what his wife did was dearer in Heaven than his devotion in selling his *tefillin* to purchase the *etrog*.

* * *

This story teaches us that the emotive response is more precious than a clearly holy *mitzvah*. This is an amazing, novel chassidic thought. Heaven told Rebbe Zusha that his calm silence was worth more than purchasing the *etrog*—and that although now he had no *etrog* and no *tefillin*, it was no matter. What matters is that he sold the *tefillin* in order to purchase the *etrog* and then he remained silent when his wife destroyed the *etrog*. In other words, it is our intention that matters—not the outcome. Rebbe Zusha trusted God. On Sukkot men do not don *tefillin*, so Rebbe Zusha sold them to fund his *etrog*. And then his wife destroyed his *etrog* but he did not feel any anger. He was still certain that all would be well.

Proud of His Children

Once, Rebbe Zusha wanted to nullify an evil decree. In order to do so, he invited all the *Ushpizin*, the seven shepherds of the holiday of Sukkot, to descend to his *sukkah* and together, they would nullify the decree. All of them did indeed descend and told Rebbe Zusha that the fact that they descended to the lower world was not because of his special unifications or the spiritual work he had done. Rather, it was in the merit of the simple service with which he served God, as a simple Jew, with self-sacrifice and effort—so much so that God sits in Heaven and says "Look at this creation that I have created. Look at my son Zusha, 'Israel through whom I am glorified.'"

* * *

The Ba'al Shem Tov has a unique explanation: That the attribute of *tiferet* (beauty) refers to serving God in a way that will cause God "amazement" — making Him proud of us.

What is God proud of? The shepherds [the Patriarchs, Moses, Aaron, Joseph, and David] later told Rebbe Zusha that they see in Heaven that the decree is actually a good one, so they cannot help him nullify it. But that since he sees it down below as evil, he should nullify it himself (and they will give him the power to do so). "We descended just to witness the creation of whom God is proud," they told Rebbe Zusha. "Not because of lofty spiritual intentions, but rather because of your simple service of God."

Rebbe Zusha's glorification of God through his simple service is a phenomenon of *netzach* and *hod* (victory and splendor). But the fact that his simple service causes God to be proud is in their inner dimension. Whether Zusha was aware of it or not, this is the service of *tiferet*. *netzach* and *hod* are the "two supporters of truth" while tiferet is the essence, the inner dimension of truth, the attribute of truth. God's amazement and pride in Rebbe Zusha are from the point of truth in his simple service. On Simchat Torah we dance with all three: *netzach* and *hod* are the two wooden poles of the Torah scroll and the *tiferet* is the Torah scroll itself…

REBBE DOVID OF LELOV: "A TIME TO BE SILENT AND A TIME TO SPEAK"

Rebbe Dovid Biderman of Lelov, the founder of the Lelov dynasty, was born in 5506 (1745) to a family that opposed Chassidut. Nonetheless, he was drawn to Chassidut from his youth. Rebbe Dovid was a disciple of Rebbe Elimelech of Lizhansk and afterward, of the Seer of Lublin. He was known for his great love of the Jewish people, for not imparting words of Torah in public and for bringing Jews close to God (among them the Admor the doctor, Rebbe Chaim Dovid Bernhard). It was he who brought the *Heilige Yid* (Rabbi Yakov Yitzchak of Parshischa) to Chassidut and ultimately sealed their relationship with a marriage between their children. His other disciples included his son, Rebbe Moshe, Rebbe Itche (Yitzchak) of Vorky, Rebbe Yeshayah of Pordborzh and Rebbe Chanoch of Warsaw. Rebbe Dovid passed away on the 7th day of Shevat 5574 (1814) and was brought to rest in Lelov, Poland.

At the end of the *shloshim* (the 30 days of mourning) for Rebbe Dovid of Lelov, his son Rebbe Moshe—who eventually made *aliyah* to the Land of Israel where he perpetuated the dynasty—and his disciple, Rebbe Itche (Yitzchak) of Vorky—journeyed to Rebbe Mordechai of Chernobyl. The two made their way to Rebbe Mordechai in order to consult with him as to which Rebbe they should adopt after the passing of Rebbe Dovid. Perhaps they even wanted to investigate whether Rebbe Mordechai, himself, should be their next mentor. Due to the distance between Chernobyl and Lelov, Rebbe Mordechai did not know Rebbe Moshe and Rebbe Yitzchak personally.

When the two entered Rebbe Mordechai's room, he began by telling them a story: Before my father, Rebbe Nachum of Chernobyl, passed away, I sat by his bed and cried profusely. My father asked me why I was crying so much. "As long as you are with me," I answered, "you have taught me Torah, from the time I was a toddler. If you leave me, who will teach me?" My father replied, "Don't worry. Even after I will be in the next world, I will come to you and continue to teach you." And so it was. My father comes to me regularly to teach me Torah. Recently, my father did not appear for thirty days. I was very worried. Perhaps I did something wrong. Why would my father stop coming to me after so many years? But this morning, my father came, thank God. "Where were you?" I asked him. "Why didn't you come for thirty days? You never stayed away this long...."

"Exactly thirty days ago," my father answered, "one of the great *tzaddikim* (pious people) who you do not know, Rebbe Dovid of Lelov, passed away. Because during his life in this world he never imparted words of Torah, in the Garden of Eden they decided to honor him for the entire thirty-day mourning period with the privilege of teaching Torah in the presence of all the *tzaddikim*. Thus, I was not able to come. Now that the thirty days are over, I have returned to you."

* * *

What do we learn from this story? There are *tzaddikim* who do not impart Torah in this world and there are *tzaddikim* (such as the Alter Rebbe of Chabad) who impart Torah with abundance. The latter are *tzaddikim* whose entire lives revolve around teaching Torah, such as Moses and the Mashiach, who will reveal a new dimension of the Torah. In this story, we discover that the *tzaddikim* who do not impart Torah are compensated, as it were, after they pass on, when they teach Torah in the Garden of Eden. Thus, it is not that they do not have Torah to teach. They do. But as far as public teaching of Torah, they are "hidden" *tzaddikim*. It is possible to be a hidden *tzaddik* in one area of life and a revealed *tzaddik* in another.

Times, Eras, and Lifetimes

This is connected to the secret of *chashmal*.[1] The sages explain that the word *chashmal* is the secret of, "at times they are silent and at times they speak," as is written in Ecclesiastes, "a time to be silent and a time to speak."[2] The literal intent of the 28 divisions of time listed in Ecclesiastes (a time to be silent, to speak, to cast away stones, to gather stones, etc.) refer to life in this world. There is a day or time in which we are called upon to be silent and there is a time for us to speak.

But the word Ecclesiastes uses for "time" (עֵת) can also mean, "an era." It can even refer to an entire lifetime or incarnation. Thus Ecclesiastes is saying that there can be an entire lifetime in which the *tzaddik* comes to the world and is in an "era of silence" (in which he still does many good things). After he

---

1. Ezekiel 1:4.
2. Ecclesiastes 3:7.

departs from the world, he enters an era in which he is called upon, "to speak." The era to speak could be in the Garden of Eden, as in the story about Rebbe Dovid of Lelov, who was given the honor to speak there. However, it would seem that just thirty days for "a time to speak" in the Garden of Eden is not enough to compensate for the silence of an entire lifetime. The *tzaddik* is then told, as we find in some stories from the Ba'al Shem Tov: "In your previous incarnation, you did not speak. You have much to say to the Jewish people, so return to this world again and in your next incarnation, speak with abundance." Indeed, one of the explanations of contraction is that it is meant to increase the flow. For example, water that is held back by a dam, when it first bursts through the barrier, flows with great strength.

"Truly God does all these twice or thrice to a man"[3]

From this, we learn that there are pairs of incarnations of a soul—one silent, one loquacious—corresponding to the secret of *chash-mal*: silence and speech. According to the Ba'al Shem Tov, the *mal* part of *chashmal* actually splits into two distinct stages, both called *mal*, which can be the source of some confusion. However, the first *mal* refers to a state of separation, following the etymology of *mal* as "circumcision" (מִילָה) and the second *mal* is the one that refers to sweetening or speech, following the etymology of *mal* as "word" (מִלָּה). So the full process includes three stages, to which the Ba'al Shem Tov usually referred as submission-separation-sweetening (הַכְנָעָה הַבְדָּלָה הַמְתָּקָה). So, now we can speak of three incarnations for each *tzaddik*.

---

3.   Job 33:29. This verse was cited by the Arizal as one of the main sources for his teachings on incarnation.

In his first incarnation, the *tzaddik* is silent. He is completely concealed. Rebbe Dovid of Lelov was a concealed *tzaddik* only in the realm of publicly imparting Torah, but there are hidden *tzaddikim* who are completely silent and totally unknown. In his second incarnation, the *tzaddik* appears as the first *mal* related to circumcision, apparently to face a trial that has to do with rectified sexual conduct. In his third incarnation, the *mal* related to speech comes to the fore. Since the *tzaddik* has already been silent, and he has already withstood various trials, he is now granted the freedom to speak and pour forth an endless stream of the sweet and living waters of Torah into the world.

Three Personas

The intermediary stage of *mal* (as in separation or circumcision) is best personified by Joseph, who had to withstand the most difficult trials related to his identity while in Egypt, particularly when Potiphar's wife tried to seduce him.[4] Joseph passes all his tests with flying colors, retaining his holy identity as a Jew amidst the decadent spiritual state of Egypt.

The archetypal silent *tzaddik* is personified in chassidic teachings with Isaac (Joseph's grandfather, who was the only one who knew that Joseph was still alive and in Egypt). Whereas Abraham journeyed and publicized faith in One God throughout the world, Isaac stayed at home, effecting Divine-spiritual unifications and digging wells. By digging those wells, he performed an act that is described in Chassidut as "raising

---

4. Sexuality is associated in Chassidut with identity. This was explained by the fifth Lubavitcher Rebbe as the reason why improper sexual conduct, even the type that is not mentioned explicitly in the Torah, is so destructive. It chips away at our fidelity to our very selves and causes havoc in our ability to pursue our mission in life, which is our true spiritual identity.

feminine waters" (הַעֲלָאַת מַיִין נוּקְבִּין), awakening people to return to God. Isaac brought people back to God, but we do not hear many words of Torah from him.

Joseph and David are very different archetypal souls. However, these archetypes complement one another, especially in the figures of Mashiach the son of Joseph and Mashiach the son of David. Joseph's self-sacrifice to preserve his identity and purity[5] *mal* reappears as David's sweet Psalms full of God's praises. As Joseph's complement, David was not required to withstand a trial similar to Joseph's. Instead, David's challenge was to repent and return to God. The King Mashiach, who will reveal a new dimension of the Torah is also a returnee to God.

Fittingly, the sum of the numerical values of these three souls, Isaac (יִצְחָק), Joseph (יוֹסֵף), and David (דָּוִד) exactly equal *chashmal* (חַשְׁמַל)!

---

5.   All Jewish leaders identified as exemplifying Mashiach, the son of Joseph dedicated their lives to strengthening the Jewish people's identity as Jews by encouraging Torah learning and the performance of God's commandments. Following the example of Joseph the *tzaddik* who did the same for the children of Israel that were in exile in Egypt, they are all called *tzaddikim*.

The Rebbe Rayatz: "We Will Meet Again"

The Rebbe Rayatz, Rabbi Yosef Yitzchak Schneerson, was the sixth Chabad Rebbe. Born to his father, the fifth Rebbe of Chabad, the Rebbe Rashab, in 5640 (1880), the Rebbe Rayatz worked tirelessly to keep Judaism alive in the Soviet Union and was jailed for his heroic efforts. Forced to leave Russia, he continued to conduct the struggle from Latvia, and then from the Warsaw Ghetto, eventually escaping the Holocaust to the United States. By the time of his passing in New York on the 10th of Shevat 5710 (1950) he had laid the foundation for the global renaissance of chassidic Jewish life in the US and throughout the world.

After the 6th Lubavitcher Rebbe, the Rebbe Rayatz was miraculously saved from the Soviet prison, he was sent to exile and from there was expelled from Russia. When the Rebbe Rayatz left Russia, at the end of Tishrei 5688 (1928), the *chassidim* came to take leave of him. Among those *chassidim* was the family of Reb Chanya Marozov. Reb Chanya himself was in Siberia, either in prison there or on a mission for the Rebbe Rayatz. Reb Chanya's young son, Reb Shalom, held onto the Rebbe and didn't want to let him go. The Rebbe said to him, "We will meet again."

* * *

Let us imagine this story: The Rebbe Rayatz is about to leave Russia. The family of Reb Chanya (Elchanan) Marozov (it is good to be familiar with the names of these people, who had tremendous self-sacrifice for their brethren), who himself is in jail or on the Rebbe's mission in Siberia to strengthen the spiritual state of his fellow Jews, has come to part with the Rebbe. There is a little boy there, Reb Shalom, whose father is in jail. For now, the Rebbe is like a father to him. While it is not good that his father is in jail, it is good that he relates to the Rebbe as his father. He is holding on to the Rebbe and does not want to let go. The Rebbe feels the little boy's pain and wants to reassure him. He confidently promises him that, "We will meet again." In those tumultuous times, when the Rebbe was leaving Russia and the Marozov family was remaining in Russia, it was no simple matter to promise the boy that they would meet again.

* * *

22 years later, the Rebbe's promise was fulfilled: Despite all the upheavals of those dark days, in Tevet 5710—just a month before the Rebbe Rayatz's passing—Reb Shalom reached the Rebbe's headquarters in New York. When he entered the Rebbe's room for his personal meeting (called *yechidut*) the Rebbe said to him, "Nu, so we meet again."

* * *

In this story, we see the Rebbe's foresight, an aspect of the attribute of wisdom, as the sages say, "Who is wise? He who sees what is to be born (the future)."[1] It is also an expression of the

---

1. *Tamid* 32a.

attribute of understanding, which is referred to as, "the coming future" and "the World to Come."[2] This refers to the future that is full of joy, just as the *sefirah* of understanding is full of joy, its inner dimension.

Another important lesson that we learn from this story: The Rebbe sees a small boy crying. He looks into his soul and knows what the child needs to hear. He knows what will calm him and promises that they will meet again. We can all learn how to relate to others in this manner. The Rebbe is not simply relating future events. He was bringing the future into the present; as it were, borrowing from the future in order to give the child strength in the present, the strength that would help him persevere until the joy of the future would be revealed.

Rebbe Nachman of Breslev said that it is greatly beneficial for a person to imagine himself with a *tzaddik*. This can save him from difficult situations and spiritual failures. The Rebbe Rayatz told the boy that they would meet again. His promise surely accompanied him and safeguarded him through all the years in Russia—until he merited seeing the Rebbe once again.

---

2.   *Eitz Chaim, Shaar* 15, chapter 5.

THE REBBE RAYATZ: ALWAYS WITH HIS CHASSIDIM

In 5707 (1947), two years after the end of World War II, Rebbetzin Chanah Schneerson, the mother of the Lubavitcher Rebbe, reached Paris on her way to the US, where she planned to live near her son. This was after she had remained with her husband, Rabbi Levi Yitzchak Schneerson, for years of forced-exile deep in Russia. Rabbi Levi Yitzchak passed away during that period of exile.

The Lubavitcher Rebbe, who at that time was the Rebbe-to-be, traveled to Paris to greet his mother, whom he had not seen for years, and to escort her to the US. The Rebbe stayed in Paris a number of months until they could set sail. During that time, the Chabad *chassidim* in Paris took advantage of the opportunity and held *farbrengens* with the Rebbe.

At one of the *farbrengens*, some of the *chassidim* asked the Rebbe to request of his father-in-law, the Rebbe Rayatz, to awaken Heavenly mercy upon them so that they would succeed in obtaining visas to leave France for America. The Rebbe looked at the very important *chassidim,* smiled a bit at their request and said, "Do you think that someone has to remind the Rebbe to think good thoughts and awaken abundant mercy upon them? I will tell you a story."

The Rebbe related the following story: Due to the Rayatz's imprisonment in a Communist jail and the terrible hardships he faced there—he was sentenced to death and was brutally tortured—he became ill. Once the Rayatz reached the US, there was a period of time during which a nurse would enter his room every morning to give him a shot. This took place daily at exactly 7 AM. The Rayatz would sit ready at his table, the nurse would knock on the door, enter and give him the shot.

Once, the nurse knocked on the Rayatz's door early, at one minute before 7. Nobody answered. She waited until 7, and then knocked again. But still no answer. She opened the door and walked in. The Rayatz was sitting, facing the door, completely awake, but with eyes closed. He looked as though he was not really there. Concerned, the nurse immediately called the Rebbetzin, who was concerned as well. Finally, they called the Rebbe to come quickly. The Rebbe put his ear near the Rayatz's mouth and could hear that he was quietly saying the Song of the Sea with its cantillation notes. The Rebbe told the nurse and family that the Rayatz was in a state of communion and disembodiment and that he was perfectly fine.

That night, twelve hours later, they received a telegram informing them that a group of the Rayatz's *chassidim* had miraculously escaped over the Russian border. If they had been caught, they would have been summarily executed. The very moments during which they managed to cross the border, with great Divine intervention, were the minutes the Rayatz was saying the Song of the Sea in his state of disembodiment.

"So," the Rebbe finished telling the *chassidim*, "know that the Rebbe is always with everyone, especially with his close *chassidim*. He is always connected to them, particularly in times of need. When a *chassid* is in trouble, the Rebbe is together with him, awakening Divine mercy upon him, as if he was grasping his hand and extricating him from danger."

* * *

This is a story of cleaving between Rebbe and *chassid* that is above reason and knowledge. Of course, any Jew can, in one moment, become a Rebbe's *chassid*. It is written that a Rebbe thinks about his *chassidim* (and doesn't only pray for them). Besides feeling them and knowing what is happening to them, he has the power to bring them out of trouble with his thought. This thought, however, is not just an intellectual type of thought. The Rebbe achieves the salvation for his *chassidim* by awakening Heavenly mercy for Divine assistance, above and beyond what could be naturally effected.

How did the Rayatz, thousands of miles away from his *chassidim,* know that they were in danger and manage to awaken mercy upon them? To awaken great mercy is to awaken the secret of the *Dikna*. The *Dikna* is the metaphoric beard of the Long Countenance (*Arich Anpin*), the lower of the two *partzufim* in the *sefirah* of crown and possesses thirteen conduits (*tikunei dikna*), which correspond to the Thirteen Principles of Divine

Mercy (Exodus 34:6-7). As such, these thirteen conduits are considered the source of God's great mercy. When a supernatural miracle is needed, the great mercy of the crown is necessary, as the more accessible mercy of the emotive powers of the small countenance (*Ze'er Anpin*) are not sufficient.

If the Rebbe told this story in response to the *chassidim's* request of the Rayatz to awaken mercy upon them, it is a sign that according to the Rebbe's "feel" for the Rayatz—and if anybody could feel the Rayatz, it was the Rebbe—the place from which the salvation came was even higher than the *Dikna* of *Arich Anpin* and its source. According to Kabbalah, the thirteen levels of rectification of the *Dikna* have two sources (to understand this, one has to study the writings of the Arizal in-depth): the concealed mind (*mocha stima'ah*), also known as the wisdom of the *sefirah* of crown, and even higher—the so-called skull (*galgalta*) which is the crown of the wisdom of the crown, also known as the great love [of the Almighty] (*ahavah rabbah*) in chassidic teachings or the will of the will.

In this story we feel the crown connection between the two sources of the *Dikna* mentioned above. When the Rebbe thinks about his *chassid*, that thought comes from the concealed mind (*mocha stima'ah*) in the crown. When he thinks about his *chassid* with great love—not only thinking about him but also loving him with infinite love—this infinite love of the Rebbe is really the right hand that is able to reach his *chassid*. The right hand is always a symbol of love but the right hand of the small countenance (*Ze'er Anpin*), can only embrace others from nearby. The verse, "And his right hand will embrace me" refers to this right hand. But, there is also the right hand of the higher part of the *sefirah* of crown called *Atik*, and this right hand is explained as being enclothed within the skull (of *Arich Anpin*). This right hand and its great love can extend to the farthest reaches of the world.

In this story, we see how the Rebbe can save those who are connected to him from danger with his limitless right hand, while he is completely focused and divested of physicality (as described in this story). The Rebbe's knowledge of what is happening with his *chassidim* is much more than mere telepathy. The Rebbe is actually there with his *chassidim*. His arm embraces them, and that is how he saves them from danger. The enclothement of the right-hand of *Atik* in the skull (of *Arich Anpin*) together with his ability to connect from afar with his concealed mind, are the two sources of the thirteen levels of rectification of the *Dikna,* from which the great mercy is drawn.

One more point that we can take with us from this story and that can benefit us all, even if we are not initiated into the teachings of the Arizal, is that there is a powerful connection between saying the Song of the Sea and awakening mercy from Heaven. If the Lubavitcher Rebbe noted this (he could have told the story without mentioning what the *Rayatz* had been saying during his disembodiment), it means that we should be aware of this. If you think about someone who needs Heavenly mercy and recite the Song of the Sea with sincerity and the proper intent, you will be awakening the Heavens to be merciful with him. This is true both for an individual and for the entire Jewish people.

Rebbe Baruch of Garelitz: Fine Distinction between Truth and Falsehood

Rebbe Baruch of Garelitz was the fifth son of Rebbe Chaim of Sanz, the 'Divrei Chaim.' He was born in 5589 (1829) to his father, Rebbe Chaim, and his mother, Rachel Faigeh, the daughter of the *'Baruch Ta'am.'* He served as a rabbi in Rodnick and Garelitz and after his father's passing, became a chassidic Rebbe. He was known for his sharp intellect, quick wit and his acute sense of truth. Rebbe Baruch passed away on the first of Adar, 5666 (1906). His son, Rebbe Elisha, succeeded him as rabbi of Garelitz, but refused to assume the mantle of a chassidic Rebbe.

Rebbe Baruch related a parable about his trait of truth and the difference between him and his brother, Rebbe Yechezkel of Shinwa: "If my big brother, Yechezkel, would see a huge mountain that is all bad, but would notice that inside it there is a good stone—he would make every effort in the world, with self-sacrifice, to reach that good stone and bring it out of the mountain (even if the mountain was a million times greater than the stone—a million times more evil than good). I, on the other hand, if I see a mountain that is all good, but that has one small stone of bad—I will throw the entire mountain into the garbage."

The Difference Between Kosher and Pure

Even as a small child, Rebbe Baruch was known for his sharp sense of distinction between evil and good. He was a small and very gifted boy, with special, refined sensitivity, who would discern things that adults did not feel.

There was a group of butchers in his town—ritual slaughterers and kosher meat marketers. One of them was aware of the special gift of the Rabbi's son, Rebbe Baruch. He asked him if he could help him choose the animals for slaughter. "Tell me which animal will be kosher and which will be unkosher," he requested of the small boy.

Before the animal is slaughtered, it is not possible to see if it will be kosher or not, as the kosher status depends upon the health of the animal's internal organs. The butchers had to buy the animal at great expense, and only after it was slaughtered would they know if they would be able to market the meat as kosher—at a greater profit. This particular butcher saw that the young Rebbe Baruch had a special perception, and promised him a coin for every animal that he would observe before he would purchase it, and tell him if the animal would be kosher or not. Little Baruch, who was happy to be able to earn some money so that he would be able to give charity, began his new "job." "This cow is kosher," he would say, "and this cow is not kosher." His predictions were always correct.

The butcher, who always knew which animal to buy, became a wealthy man. His colleagues finally asked him what his secret was. "How could it be that every animal that you choose is kosher?"

"The Rebbe's young son tells me which animal is kosher and which is not," he answered.

"This is not fair," the butchers protested. "Why should you have inside information?" The butchers' protests reached the Rebbe's ears. He called his son and asked him how he knew which animal would be kosher. His son answered innocently, "It is not *ruach hakodesh* (Divine inspiration), but actually very simple. I look at how the animal walks in the street. An animal with its head raised in haughtiness is not kosher, while an animal that walks with its head down, modestly, is kosher."

* * *

Lowly Spirit

This is a beautiful story about the innocent sense of a young boy—albeit a boy with a lofty and pure soul and a great measure of Heavenly help, as he was the son of a *tzaddik*. But we can also learn a lesson that is applicable to all: Someone who walks haughtily (as written in the Code of Jewish Law)—shows that something inside his soul is not right—that he is not spiritually healthy. A person who walks modestly, with his head down, is a sign of a kosher Jew. This is a very important story about Rebbe Baruch of Gurelitz.

There are other stories about the young Rebbe Baruch seeing angels. We usually do not see angels (perhaps there are children who do…). Rebbe Baruch described the angels as being large, reaching from earth to heaven. As in the story above, Rebbe Baruch could also distinguish between good angels, who come to help us perform *mitzvahs* and who safeguard us from transgressing—and destructive angels. How could he tell? In the same way. He said that if the angel walks slowly, modestly, it is clear that he is an angel that came from heaven to do good for someone, because he possesses humility and lowliness. If, on the other hand, the angel conducts himself with strength and aggressiveness, and while walking he tears and breaks things, it is obvious that he is a destructive angel, a bad angel.

How can we understand Rebbe Boruch's saying that he would be willing to throw out an entire mountain of good just because of one small point of bad? There are different types of *tzaddikim,* as is explained in the *Tanya.* One of the main ways that the perfection of the *tzaddik* is tested is in his absolute hatred for evil. When it looks like something is almost completely good, but it does contain a small amount of evil—this point of evil is a sign that the good is not true and absolute. As the *Tanya* explains, a non-consummate *tzaddik* still has some bad. He is a "*tzaddik* who has bad," and this is not what God desires. Rebbe Baruch was a consummate *tzaddik.* Even when everything looked good—if there was a drop of evil mixed in, he did not need and would not want the item at all.

There are many stories about *maggids* and angels who revealed themselves to people, taught them Torah and disclosed secrets to them. The distinction between a *maggid* who belongs on the side of holiness or God forbid, to the Other Side is along the same lines. Even if this *maggid* reveals many true, wondrous secrets to the person, if there is one small point of falsehood or evil, (a false revelation or a directive that conflicts with Torah and its *mitzvahs*)—that is proof that all of this *maggid's* revelations must be rejected, and that he is completely on the other side.

We can connect Rebbe Baruch's strong stance on complete truth to the stories of his ability to make fine distinctions. A person who is stringent about the pure truth, without any point of falsehood, even as a child can naturally distinguish between good and evil, a kosher animal and a non-kosher animal, and a good angel and an angel of destruction. Maimonides, who explains that all the traits in the Torah require walking down the middle path, determines that any hint of pride must be completely negated. Truth must be pure of any adulteration of falsehood. The greatest falsehood is pride. Thus, Moses ("Moses and his Torah are truth"[1]) is also the "most humble man on the face of the earth."[2]

---

1. *Bava Batra* 74a.
2. Numbers 12:3.

REBBE LEIB SARAH'S: THE LOAN THAT MADE A MARRIAGE

Rebbe Leib Sarah's was one of the most wondrous *tzaddikim* in the annals of Chassidut. He was born in 5490 (1729) and apparently was named after the Maharal of Prague from whom he descended. He was called "Sarah's" after his righteous mother, Sarah. When she was a young woman, the local landowner wanted to force her to marry him. In order to foil his plan, she immediately married Reb Yosef, a poor, elderly teacher. She knew that her husband was a hidden *tzaddik* and asked him to bless her that she should have a holy son like him. And so, Rebbe Leib was born. When he was 15 years old, he became a disciple of the Ba'al Shem Tov and later, of the Maggid of Mezritch. Throughout his life, Rebbe Leib wandered throughout the world, searching for Jews who were suffering troubles or were in captivity, helping them in a wondrous manner. He had the ability to command any person—no matter what his lofty station in life—to do whatever he directed him to do. Reb Leib Sarah's passed away on the fourth of Adar 5551 (1791).

A certain young man wanted to become a disciple of Rebbe Leib Sarah's. He constantly asked Reb Leib's disciples to intercede on his behalf, but try as he might, Rebbe Leib would not accept him. Finally, he said that if the young man would be willing to sell all of his property to loan him the money for a year, then he would agree for him to join his group of disciples. The young man accepted the condition, sold all of his property and lent all the money to Rebbe Leib.

He happily sat in the study hall and learned Torah with the group of Rebbe Lieb's disciples.

When the year was up, Rebbe Leib came to the young man with part of the loan and said to him: "Give me the loan document and write me a new document in accordance with the money that I am returning to you now. With this money, go out and buy respectable clothing, rent a carriage and a driver, travel to Kovna and tell the matchmaker there that you would like to propose marriage to Miss X. Give him a large sum for his trouble and then see what happens next.

The young man did as he was told, arrived in Kovna and spoke with the matchmaker, who laughed in his face: "Miss X is a beautiful, extremely wealthy and extremely intelligent orphan. She runs all of her business in the city by herself. This is why she has not found a match as of yet. Who are you compared to her?"

The young man gave the matchmaker a large coin and said to him: "What difference does it make to you? Try!"

The matchmaker agreed to try and after Shabbat, approached Miss X and said to her, "A certain Jew has come to Kovna. I don't even know him. But I have to make my living and he gave me a substantial sum of money so that I would propose that you marry him."

"Please find out more about this young man and get back to me," Miss X answered.

The matchmaker, who was surprised that Miss X did not immediately reject his proposal, went to do some research about the young man and returned to her with his name and other relevant details.

"I agree to marry him," she said. But to save face, tell him to rent six stores next to mine and open a shopping center. I will order merchandise that will come under his name. When people see that he is a wealthy man, it will not be embarrassing for me to marry him and all will work out."

When the young man rented the stores (with money provided by his bride-to-be) her assistants came and told her that her new neighbor is growing and may be a potential threat to her business. "No matter," she answered them. "Leave him alone. Perhaps he will not be selling the same merchandise that I sell." But when the merchandise arrived, it was the very same as hers and very high quality. Once again, the assistants warned her of her new competitor and she ignored them. After some time, she said to her uncle, "Perhaps you can do some research on this new merchant? I heard that he is single." The uncle quickly did the research and the marriage was arranged.

Two years after their wedding, the husband and wife were sitting and talking. The wife bent over for a moment and precisely then, Rebbe Leib Sarah's entered their home, placed the rest of the money that he owed his disciple on the table, asked for the loan document and left. The wife saw Rebbe Leib on his way out and said to her husband, "Go out to accompany him. That is Rebbe Leib!"

"How do you know Rebbe Leib?" asked the husband, surprised.

"Why do you think I agreed to marry you?" she answered. "Some time before you arrived in Kovna, an old man came to me time and again. He said that his name was Leib the son of Sarah. He told me that I have to marry a certain young man, that he is my soulmate. My deceased father also came to me in a dream and told me to listen to Rebbe Leib, but I didn't listen. Finally, I became deathly ill and then I took upon myself to listen to Rebbe Leib. So when you arrived in Kovna, all that I had to do was to inquire as to your name and then accepted the proposal…

* * *

Most people prefer to be on the side of the lender and not on the side of the borrower. After all, who wants to be indebted to someone else? But Rebbe Leib had his reasons and he particularly liked to borrow money. He preferred to borrow and return money as opposed to receiving money as a donation, called a *pidyon*, from his followers, as was the accepted mode of income for *tzaddikim*. Rebbe Leib would say that the money that he received as a loan was certainly acceptable by Torah law—which may possibly not have been the case if a person gave money to a *tzaddik* so that he would pray for him, and it could be that he would also have been saved with his own prayer for himself.

There are many stories that describe how Rebbe Leib borrowed money from Jews and it ultimately turned out, as in our story, that it was not exactly a loan, but rather, a gateway to wealth. Once Rebbe Leib borrowed all the money that a particular wealthy man in his town had, and immediately afterward, a huge fire broke out and destroyed almost everything in the town. Rebbe Leib was able to return the money to the man and he was then able to rehabilitate his own business and help all of his neighbors, as well.

Even though he could have achieved the results that he wanted in a different way, Rebbe Leib wanted to "belong" to the Jew from whom he borrowed money and to enter into the deal with all seriousness. The chassidic saying is usually just the opposite, highlighting how the *chassid* belongs to his Rebbe. But Rebbe Leib reveals a deeper dimension to us, in which the leader is the servant of his people.

By borrowing money, Rebbe Leib also gained the special *mitzvah* of returning a loan, which has no personal gain and is totally for the sake of Heaven. Particularly if, as was the case with Rebbe Leib, he enjoyed owing money. It is with the power of this *mitzvah* that he was able to make matches. This is because every match includes an element of returning a heavenly loan to the soul that is missing its second half.

Another connection of Rebbe Leib to this unusual match is through his parents: A young, beautiful woman employs great self-sacrifice and willingly marries an elderly, poor teacher. We can say that Rebbe Leib saw in the couple in this story a spark of his father and mother and for that reason, he devoted himself to their match. Rebbe Nachman of Breslov writes that the initial letters of the words (Malachi 2:7), "The priest's lips safeguard knowledge and Torah" (שִׂפְתֵי כֹהֵן יִשְׁמְרוּ דַעַת וְתוֹרָה) spell out the word for "a match" (שידוך). Rebbe Leib, the righteous Kohen, keeps the knowledge of his parents, which is the connection between them—and with that inspiration, makes matches for his disciples.

Rebbe Ze'ev Wolf of Cherni-Ostra'ah: Keep Your Eyes Open and See Mashiach

Rebbe Ze'ev Wolf of Cherni-Ostra'ah was a disciple of the Maggid of Mezritch and Rebbe Meshulam Feivush of Zabriz. He was the Rabbi and Admo''r of Cherni-Ostra'ah in Ukraine.

In the year 5558 (1798), about twenty years after the first great chassidic *aliyah* to the Land of Israel, Rebbe Ze'ev Wolf made *aliyah* to Israel, settling first in Haifa and afterward in Tiberias. After the passing of Rebbe Avraham of Kalisk, Rebbe Ze'ev Wolf was appointed to be the leader of the *Chassidim*. Rebbe Ze'ev Wolf's students included Rebbe Menachem Mendel of Kosov–the father of the Vizhnitz dynasty–and Rebbe David Shlomo of Eibschitz, author of "*Arvei Nachal.*" He passed away on the fifth of Adar, 5583 (1823) and was laid to rest in Tiberias, in the section of the disciples of the Ba'al Shem Tov.

Guidance for a Simple Jew who Attained Spiritual Heights

A simple man with no special spiritual aptitude withstood a great trial. (The type of trial he withstood is not recorded. Generally, however, 'a great trial' refers to a trial in maintaining sexual purity, as in the trial of Joseph). In reward, Heaven granted him a special gift: Whenever he would mention God's Name, such as when praying or reciting a blessing, he would feel

God's majesty in his soul. As a result, whenever this man would utter a prayer or make a blessing, his entire body would begin to tremble and he would feel that his organs were burning up in fear.

There are stories about *tzaddikim* who merited lofty heights and did not want them. Rebbe Zusha of Anapoli merited to see Heaven like the Rambam and was not able to contain it. It is told of the Rebbe of Komarna that every time that he learned what one of the sages in the Talmud taught, he would see that sage before him. The teaching of the Jerusalem Talmud that when a person learns Talmud, it is as if the sage who taught that particular teaching stands before him—spontaneously occurred to him. But the Rebbe of Komarna asked God to take that spiritual level away from him, as it disturbed his study.

Our simple Jew, who did not understand why he would be experiencing such lofty spiritual heights, came to the Rebbe of Cherni-Ostra'ah and complained that he did not know what happened to him, but he could not bear the suffering it entailed. He entreated the Rebbe to help him to disengage from this spiritual level.

Rebbe Ze'ev Wolf said to him: "You have merited and were given something that others ask for and toil for their entire lives. All the *tzaddikim* serve God all their lives with an inner desire to reach this level, and you have received it as a gift. How can you forgo it? The Rebbe then proceeded to teach him how to live with this lofty level.

Rebbe Ze'ev Wolf did not agree to take this level away from the simple Jew. If he merited it, he was apparently deserving. Instead, the Rebbe gave him the tools to serve God at that level. The Ba'al Shem Tov would also take simple Jews and invest years teaching them Torah and service of God until they attained spiritual heights.

Anticipating Mashiach

Rebbe Ze'ev Wolf's eyes were always open, even when he was reciting the *Amidah*, the Silent Prayer. It is also told of Rebbe Levi Yitzchak of Berditchev that he would pray with open eyes—even in front of an open window facing the street—despite the law that says that if one is praying without a prayer book, he should close his eyes. Rebbe Levi Yitzchak said that even though his eyes were open in prayer, he did not see the comings and goings in the street. A *tzaddik* has a level of sight that is not physical. He radiates Godliness from his eyes. He sees only the Godliness in all the things taking place in front of him. In the same vein, it is also told of the first Lubavitcher Rebbe, Rebbe Shneor Zalman of Liadi, that before he died, he said that he did not see the beam in the ceiling at all, but rather the word of God giving it vitality.

Even when Rebbe Ze'ev Wolf was sleeping his eyes would remain open. We can learn from this that his soul root was the *mazal* of fish, which coincides with his day of passing in the month of Adar.

Once, Rebbe Ze'ev Wolf was laying down with his eyes closed. His assistant, who was next to his bed, thought that he had passed away and began to wail loudly. The holy rabbi opened his eyes and asked him, "Why are you crying?"

"I thought that you had passed on to heaven," the assistant answered.

"Do not fear," Rebbe Ze'ev Wolf calmed him. "We are fine. I simply closed my eyes in order to contemplate the generation of Mashiach: Our forefathers in Egypt were sunk into the depths of the 49th gate of impurity. They could not tarry in Egypt any longer, for they had nearly sunk to the fiftieth gate of impurity, from which they would not have been able to emerge. The fiftieth gate is *apikorsus* (denial of Torah), may God save us. I saw that before Mashiach comes, this gate—the impurity of *apikorsus*—will spread throughout the world, may God save us, and even for people of our stature (even *tzaddikim*, disciples of the Ba'al Shem Tov) it will be difficult to be saved from it. The solution is to speak about *tzaddikim*. This is the only force with which they can be saved from a trace of denial of Torah."

When the holy Ruzhiner Rebbe told this story, he concluded by saying, "It is even good to relate something about me, and even about my possessions, the chairs and tables." The Ruzhiner Rebbe conducted a royal court and engaged in injecting Godliness into his material possessions. This level is fitting for someone who lives at the level of "with all your might," who infuses his physical possessions and all that surrounds him with Godliness.

Opening Eyes with Stories of Tzaddikim

To see and understand the tribulations of the exile and the approach of Mashiach, Rebbe Ze'ev Wolf had to close his eyes and see the darkness. This is similar to the Covenant of the Shards that God made with Abraham: "And behold, a dread, a great darkness falls upon him,"[1] The famous Biblical commentator, Rashi, explains as follows: "This is an allusion to the troubles and darkness of the exiles." The Lubavitcher Rebbe commented that in the time of *ikvata d'Mishicha*, when the Mashiach is approaching, we are in the throes of "double and doubly-double darkness." This darkness is so pervasive that it can be tangibly felt, similar to the plague of darkness in Egypt. The Rebbe said, however, that in order to emerge from the exile, all that we have to do is "open our eyes" and see that Mashiach is rapidly approaching.

How can we open our eyes and see redemption? By telling stories of *tzaddikim*. It is written in the *Tanya* that there is a spark of Moses, a true *tzaddik,* in every Jew. The Hebrew word for "story," *sippur*, is cognate to *sapir*, "sapphire." By telling stories of *tzaddikim,* we illuminate the spark of the *tzaddik* inside us—the root of pure faith. We are then saved from the impure husk of denial of the Torah and we merit the resurrection of the dead.

---

1.   Genesis 15:12.

REBBE ELIMELECH OF LIZHENSK: GROWING BEYOND THE CRADLE

Rebbe Elimelech of Lizhensk, author of the *"Noam Elimelech,"* was the brother of Rebbe Zusha of Anipoli. Rebbe Elimelech was born to his father, Eliezer Lipa and his mother Mirel in 5477 (1717). Following in his brother, Rebbe Zusha's footsteps, Rebbe Elimelech became one of the greatest disciples of the Maggid of Mezritch. His book was known as, "the book of the righteous" and Rebbe Elimelech himself was called "the little Ba'al Shem Tov." In many ways, Rebbe Elimelech fashioned the chassidic ways of Poland in its entirety, delineating the persona of the *tzaddik* and the way to connect to him. His disciples were the chassidic masters of the next generation. Rebbe Elimelech passed away on the 21st of Adar, 5547 (1787) in Lizhensk. His son, Rabbi Eliezer, served as a rabbi after his father's passing, but did not assume the mantle of Rebbe.

Rabbi Shmuel's daughter was already 18 years old, but since she was a baby, she had not grown physically. At the age of 18, she still looked like a baby in her cradle, and spent all her days there. One day, Rabbi Shmuel's wife told him that she had heard that there was a *tzaddik*, Rebbe Elimelech, who apparently lived the closest to them of all the great *tzaddikim*. She begged her husband to journey to the *tzaddik* with their daughter. Perhaps he would be able to perform a miracle for her.

Rabbi Shmuel was not interested in *tzaddikim* or

chassidim and he certainly did not want to make the journey to see Rebbe Elimelech. For a long time, he turned a deaf ear to his wife's entreaties. Eventually, however, she wore down his opposition and he reluctantly packed his daughter into his wagon and they were off to Lizhensk, to see Rebbe Elimelech.

On the way, Rabbi Shmuel met a childhood friend, who also opposed Chassidut. The friend, who knew Rabbi Shmuel as a Torah scholar who toiled over his Torah study day and night and was meticulous with his time asked him where he was going. Rabbi Shmuel told his friend the entire story and the friend answered him, amazed, "What? You believe in Rebbes? It is a waste of time that could better be used for Torah study!" That convinced Rabbi Shmuel, and he turned around and went home. After a few weeks, Rabbi Shmuel's wife once again begged him to go to see Rebbe Elimelech. "God is great," she said to him. "He could perform a miracle. And there are *tzaddikim*. Perhaps our salvation will come through this *tzaddik*?" Rabbi Shmuel set out once again with his daughter in tow.

The two entered Rebbe Elimelech's chamber for their private conversation with him. Rebbe Elimelech told the father to place his daughter on the bed. The girl rested on the bed and Rebbe Elimelech began discussing Torah with Rabbi Shmuel.

Suddenly, in the middle of their discussion, Rebbe Elimelech turned to the girl and exclaimed, "What *chutzpah* you have to lie on my bed. Get up right now!" To the absolute amazement of her father, the girl immediately stood on her feet. She miraculously walked over to the table—but she was still tiny. "Come and I will bless you," said Rebbe Elimelech. He placed his holy hands above her head and began to bless her with an abundance of blessings. While doing so, he lifted his hands again and again further above her head. As he raised his hands, the girl grew. This continued until Rabbi Shmuel finally said, "Rebbe, I think she is tall enough now." All of this took only a few moments.

Rebbe Elimelech turned to the delighted father and said, "Now that your daughter is 18 years old, she needs to marry. Go home and make the best match that you can for her. True, you do not have money. I will write a note for you. After you make the match, go to a particular place and meet a particular person. Give him the note, which says that he should pay for all your expenses for the wedding."

After witnessing all the miracles, Rabbi Shmuel was a true believer. He went home with the intention of making a fine match for his daughter. On his way, he searched for the person who was supposed to pay for the wedding expenses. He finally found him and gave him Rebbe Elimelech's note. When the man saw the note, he removed a large bundle of money from his pocket and without thinking twice gave it to Rabbi Shmuel.

The man did not look wealthy at all. "Where is the money from?" Rabbi Shmuel asked. "My landlord threw me, my wife and children into the pit because I couldn't make my rental payments. Every day, they would throw us a piece of bread so that we wouldn't die. One day, the landlord came to the pit and I shouted to him, 'What do you gain if I am in the pit? Let me out and I will collect money from kind Jews until I can pay my debt and you will release my family.' The landlord understood that this was a better option and released me. I gathered the sum that I owe the landlord—which was exactly the sum in Rebbe Elimelech's note—and now I am on my way back home to redeem my wife and children from the pit."

Immediately after giving Rabbi Shmuel the money, this Jew set out to Rebbe Elimelech. "What will I do now?" he asked his Rebbe. "How will I save my wife and children?" "It will be fine," Rebbe Elimelech reassured him. At that moment, the landlord died and the entire family was released from the pit.

* * *

Beyond the miracles performed in this story by Rebbe Elimelech, who did in a few moment's time what nobody else had managed to do for eighteen years, the real wonder here is this Jew's complete faith in the *tzaddik*. He had so much self-nullification and lowliness that he was completely willing to give the very sum that would save his family to Rabbi Shmuel.

The entire Congregation of Israel needs a miracle like that, which will elevate Israel until it reaches its true stature. Many years have passed, but we have remained trapped in small-mindedness, incapable of thinking beyond the confines of the cradle. If we believe in the Mashiach with perfect simplicity, he will elevate the Nation of Israel to lead the entire world in God's ways—until the marriage of the Holy, blessed One and the *Shechinah*, may it be speedily in our days.

REBBE CHAIM OF AMDOR: A BEAUTIFUL LANTERN

Rebbe Chaim of Amdor, or Rebbe Chayke, as he is called was known as an ascetic and a *tzaddik* even before he became a disciple of the Maggid of Mezritch. Rebbe Chayke passed away on the 23rd day of Adar, 5547 (1787). His teachings were recorded by his followers and were published over a hundred years after his passing in a volume titled Chaim Vachesed (Warsaw 1891).

Once the Maggid spoke of a beautiful and perfect lantern that resides in Amdor; it is full of oil, has a wick, but is lacking a match to light it. The Maggid sent his foremost disciples led by Rebbe Aharon the Great of Karlin in order to meet Rebbe Chayke and draw him to the path of Chassidut.

When Rebbe Aharon and the others arrived in Amdor they made their way to the *Beit Midrash* (study hall) and there found Rebbe Chayke learning Torah with great intensity. Rebbe Aharon approached him and asked, "What are you doing?"

Rebbe Chayke answered, "I am studying Torah for its own sake."

"If so," countered Rebbe Aharon, "where are all the great gifts promised by Rabbi Me'ir in the mishnah in *Avot*?"[1]

Rebbe Chayke was taken aback by Rebbe Aharon's question while Rebbe Aharon quickly left the *Beit Midrash*. Rebbe Chayke decided he needed to speak more with Rebbe Aharon and quickly followed him, hardly catching up with him. When he did, he asked him, "So what can one do?"

Rebbe Aharon replied, "Come with me, we are traveling to Mezritch."

When they arrived, the Maggid took a figurative match and lit Rebbe Chayke. This is how Rebbe Chayke was brought to Chassidut and to the Maggid.

Years later, Rebbe Chayke related that prior to meeting the Maggid he had already fasted a number of times from Shabbat to Shabbat and had stayed up a thousand nights, engaged in Torah study and serving the Almighty, but he had not had a taste of Divine service before meeting the Maggid.

Between Amdor and Chabad

Rebbe Chayke was a friend of Rabbi Schneor Zalman of Liadi, the Alter Rebbe and founder of Chabad. Once the Mittler Rebbe, the Alter Rebbe's son happened to see a *chassid* (disciple)

---

1.   Rabbi Me'ir says, He who learns Torah for its own sake, receives many gifts. Moreover, with his learning, he justifies the existence of the entire world. He is called a friend, beloved, one who loves the Almighty, one who loves people…. (*Avot* 6:1).

of Rebbe Chayke praying with great intensity and devotion and was deeply impressed by the sincerity of his service. The Mittler Rebbe was somewhat astonished; how could there be a Jew, who was a disciple of another Rebbe, not his father's, who could pray with such devotion? He went to his father and asked him frankly, "How can an individual pray in such a manner without having studied the teachings of Chabad?"

The Alter Rebbe answered with his usual melody (the Alter Rebbe always spoke with a melody, as if he was singing a song): "It is not him praying. It is his master, Rebbe Chayke Amdorer praying." In other words, this disciple of Rebbe Chayke was praying not with his own abilities, but with his teacher's devotion. "And our goal," continued the Alter Rebbe, "is that you learn how to pray and not your Rebbe pray through you."

This is the main difference between the spiritual path taught by the great *tzaddikim* of Poland and the path taught by the Lubavitcher Rebbes. Both require the follower to devote himself to his master, but in Lubavitch the goal is to attain an independent ability to serve God.

Continues to Burn

At Rebbe Chayke's funeral, Rebbe Zusha (Rebbe Elimelech's older brother) said, "When he was alive, we did not recognize who Rebbe Chayke was. We thought he was merely a human being, but in truth he was a *seraph*,[2] an angel of burning fire. Let me tell you that even now he continues to burn before the Almighty."

---

2.   One of his teachings on the secret of the *seraphim* was taught and explained in length in this same *farbrengen* and then published as a pamphlet.

The Rebbe Rashab:
How to Connect to a Rebbe

Rebbe Shalom Dov Ber Schneerson (the Rashab), the fifth Lubavitcher Rebbe, was the founder of the Lubavitch yeshiva network, Tomchei Temimim and was called 'the Rambam of Chassidut.' He was born on the 20th of Cheshvan in 5621 (November, 1860) and passed away on the second of Nissan, 5680 (1920). He was laid to rest in Rostov in Russia.

When the Rebbe Rashab became the new leader of Chabad, at a young age, one of the elder *chassidim*, who had previously been a follower of the Rashab's father, the Rebbe Maharash and perhaps even of his grandfather, the *Tzemach Tzedek*, as well, wanted to connect on a soul level to the new rebbe. Not everyone can approach the Rebbe freely, but this *chassid* approached the young Rebbe and said, "I want to connect to you like a *chassid*. How is this done?"

The Rebbe Rashab gave him a simple answer. At that time, books of Chassidut were a bit of a rarity. Printed books were few and far between. The discourses given by the Rebbes on a regular basis were not immediately printed. They were, however, copied by a scribe. Anybody who wanted his own copy would pay the scribe a few coins and he would copy the discourse for him. "It is very inexpensive to buy a written copy of my discourses," he said. "There is a scribe here and he takes just a few coins for each copy. The correct way to connect to me is to buy the discourses and learn them well. A *chassid* learns in-depth, focusing his thought and contemplating on the content of the discourse. By studying and contemplating my teachings, as they are written, you will connect to me."

* * *

This is an extremely important principle: In order to connect to a *tzaddik*, explains the Rebbe Rashab, we have to study his teachings as they pertain to our souls. The study of Chassidut is not just the acquisition of knowledge. We must learn how the teachings apply to us personally, to help us to refine our character and to rectify our own souls. This type of Torah learning is called *"aliba d'nafshei"* (literally, "according to his own soul").—The learning has to be such that it will help me in my personal service of God. We must learn with inner, personal contemplation. By doing so, we will connect to the Rebbe.

The Addition of the Rebbe Rayatz

The Rebbe Rashab's son, the Rebbe Rayatz, answered a similar question, and his answer was printed in the *Hayom Yom*, (a daily calendar with short, focused thoughts for each day of the year) for the twenty fourth of Sivan. The *chassid*, who lived far from the Rebbe and did not merit to be near him or see him, asked how to connect to the Rebbe. The Rebbe Rayatz gave the *chassid* his father's answer—learn the discourses and read my teachings—but added two additional points:

> "First, hold *farbrengens*—joyous chassidic gatherings in which the Rebbe's teachings are discussed—with other *chassidim* in your area. Second, fulfill my directives. The Rebbe was referring mainly to reciting Psalms daily according to the daily portion and reciting the entire book of Psalms on the Shabbat preceding Rosh Chodesh, studying the Book of *Tanya* according to its daily portion, and reciting the Torah portion of the week according to its daily portion with Rashi from the *Chumash*. This is called *Chitat*: *Chumash, Tehillim* (Psalms) *Tanya*. "By fulfilling my directives, holding *farbrengens* with other *chassidim* and learning my discourses and teachings—you connect to me," the Rebbe promised.

The Rebbe's Addition

The last Lubavitcher Rebbe, Rebbe Menachem Mendel Schneerson, made another addition:

> He said that whoever wants to be his *chassid*, whoever wants to be connected to him, must spread the word of the redemption throughout the world. This is a message that is connected to the month of Nissan, which is also the month of the Rebbe's birthday.
>
> All the *tzaddikim* of all the generations have taken action for the coming of Mashiach, but in the past three generations, this action has greatly increased. When a goal is close to being fulfilled, more intense

action is required. This intense action began with the Rebbe Rashab. In every generation and at all times, the anticipation for the Mashiach heightens. The Rebbe emphasized that Mashiach is coming soon and that we must spread the word and prepare the entire world to receive Mashiach and the true and complete redemption.

* * *

Studying for Oneself and Spreading the Word

There is an important concept in Kabbalah and Chassidut: "Their end is wedged into the beginning, which means that the end comes back and connects" to the beginning. The beginning was the Rebbe Rashab, who said that the main connection between a *chassid* and the Rebbe is when the *chassid* studies the Rebbe's chassidic discourses for his own rectification. By connecting the beginning with the end we see that today, in our generation, we have to learn the Rebbe's words for our own rectification and spread his message. It is no longer enough just to learn for our personal rectification.

The Torah is light. The teachings of Chassidut taught by the Rebbe are certainly a great light. But if I learn only for myself—even if I am learning for my personal rectification—the study is still defined as "light that illuminates itself." Instead, we must take that light, which first has to illuminate itself, and transform it into "Light that illuminates others." The initials of the phrase "Light that illuminates itself" (אור המאיר לעצמו) spell the word "tent" (אהל). The same is true of the phrase: "Light that illuminates others" (אור המאיר לזולתו).

Jacob, the pillar of Torah , is described as "dwelling in tents". Whoever engages in Torah study is called a "dweller of tents." There are thus two tents: The first tent is the light that illuminates itself, in which we merit Torah learning as per the directives of the Rebbe Rashab. But we must also connect with the Rebbe using the second tent, by transforming the light of Torah into light that illuminates others.

In this way, the redemption will come speedily, in our days!

The Rebbe Rashab:
The Essence of Sincerity

Once a major meeting of rabbis was planned in Petersburgh to discuss the burning issues of the day and their impact on the Jews of the region. All the great Torah scholars of the generation attended. Among them were the Rebbe Rashab representing the *chassidim* and Rabbi Chaim of Brisk, representing the Lithuanian stream of Judaism. A preparatory meeting was called for the Sunday before the meeting in one of the towns. The Rebbe Rashab, accompanied by one of his senior *chassidim*, reached the town before Shabbat. They found an inn, the Rebbe prayed with the congregation at the local synagogue and all the while, they did not reveal the Rebbe's identity to anyone.

On Sunday, Rabbi Chaim of Brisk arrived in town. Everyone heard of the arrival of the Torah giant and went out to welcome him. Rabbi Chaim, who knew that the Rebbe Rashab was already there, asked where the Lubavitcher Rebbe was staying; but nobody knew. Only after some investigation did they understand that the guest who had prayed at the synagogue over Shabbat was none other than the Lubavitcher Rebbe, himself. "How could it be that the Lubavitcher Rebbe was staying here and you did not know?" Rabbi Chaim rebuked the townspeople.

In those days, in emergency situations for the Jews, all the Torah leaders would gather together to search for a solution. The great *chassidim* and great Lithuanian rabbis would come together with love for one another. Not only that, but Rabbi Chaim of Brisk would always completely adopt the Rebbe Rashab's opinion. This raised more than a few eyebrows among the rabbis there. "Why do you always concur with the Lubavitcher Rebbe's opinion? What authority does he have for you?" they asked Rabbi Chaim. "All of the Lubavitcher Rebbe's pockets are filled with self-sacrifice," Rabbi Chaim of Brisk answered. When self-sacrifice is needed, he just inserts his hand into his pocket and pulls some out. Do you think that I should not listen to a person with so much self-sacrifice? Do you think that I should not answer amen to his opinion?"

* * *

From this story, we can learn about sincerity and earnestness (*temimut*)—an attribute that the Rebbe Rashab, the founder of the *Tomchei Temimim* yeshivas, highlighted as the core attribute of Chassidut.

The Alter Rebbe said that one must "live with the times," with the Torah portion of the week. The sages connect the first verse in the Torah portion of *Chayei Sarah*, "And the life of Sarah was one hundred years and twenty years and seven years, the years of the life of Sarah," with the verse in Psalms (37:8), "God knows the days of the sincere (*temimim*)." They explain that "just as they are sincere, so their years are sincere and whole. At twenty years old Sarah was beautiful as a seven-year-old; at one-hundred years old she was like a twenty-year-old regarding sin." A number of commentaries ask a question about this explanation (which is also quoted by *Rashi*): Is a seven-year-old more beautiful than a twenty-year-old? On the surface, just the opposite is true!

The commentaries explain something very important, which is the inner meaning of the explanation of, "God knows the days of *temimim*" regarding Sarah, the first *temimah*. They explain that a seven-year-old does not know that she is beautiful, and thus, her beauty is simply sincere. Her beauty is part of her natural consciousness. She is not conscious of herself. She did not yet eat of the Tree of Knowledge and is not conceited. She does not stand in front of the mirror thinking how pretty she is. If a young woman of twenty is still not conscious of her beauty, we say that "twenty years old like a seven-year-old." This explanation best defines the attribute of *temimut*, sincerity.

When we understand the attribute of *temimut* in this manner, we see that it proves to be the rectification of the sin of the Tree of Knowledge, Eve's sin, which injected mankind with excessive self-consciousness. Thus, Sarah rectified Eve's sin.

According to Jewish law, a man should not look in a mirror as part of the prohibition against men wearing women's attire. A woman, however, is allowed to look in the mirror. Some commentaries explain that a woman is allowed to have self-consciousness, which is prohibited for a man. But here we see the opposite: When a righteous woman, like Sarah, looks in the mirror she experiences a divestment of physicality. She is not conscious of herself (which is not true of a man who looks in the mirror). A righteous woman can even put on makeup without consciousness of self. This is the true beauty of a daughter of Israel, the beauty of "God knows the days of the *temimim*."

One of the great Torah scholars of the later generations, the Maharam Schiff, explains the praise for a bride, "A beautiful and graceful bride," in the same manner. What is her grace? He explains that she is not conscious of her beauty, it is wholesome beauty.

When we do not have self-consciousness, we are sincere and not looking to stand out (*blitot* or "bumps," in the language of Chassidut). Even if nobody recognizes us (as was the case with the Rebbe Rashab in the town), it is just fine.

REBBE AHARON OF KARLIN: PLEASURE IN SERVICE OF GOD

Rebbe Aharon Hagadol of Karlin was one of the great disciples of the Maggid of Mezritch and one of the great disseminators of Chassidut in Lithuania. He was known for his enthusiastic service of God, praying in a loud voice (as the Karlin *chassidim* continue to do until today). His infectious charisma and palpable pleasure in the service of God brought tens of thousands of Jews back to Judaism. Rebbe Aharon also authored the famous poem *Kah echsof.* He passed away on the 19th of Nissan 5532 (1772) at the age of 36 and is buried in Karlin in Belarus. His descendants and disciples established the chassidic courts of Karlin, Ludmir, Lechovitch, Cubrin, Slonim and Koidinov.

Rebbe Aharon's special delight in service of God is exemplified in the following story:

Once, on Shabbat night, the Maggid of Mezritch was resting. (The holy books explain the loftiness of sleeping on Shabbat night). Rebbe Aharon was lying on a bench in the Study Hall of Mezritch. It looked like he was sleeping, but in truth, he was quietly reciting the Song of Songs. As he continued, the Maggid's aide entered the study hall and told Rebbe Aharon that the Maggid requested of him to stop saying the Song of Songs. His heartfelt pleasure was creating commotion and excitement in all the upper worlds and the Maggid couldn't fall asleep!

When Rebbe Hillel of Paritch would tell this story, he would cry, saying that despite the loftiness of Rebbe Aharon's Song of Songs, which created great commotion in all the upper worlds, the Maggid's sleep was even greater than that.

* * *

We see that Rebbe Aharon had a special 'sense' for the Song of Songs. It is specifically a person with such a sense—who can feel the intense power and pleasure of service of God in holiness—who can bring people who have fallen into sin because of their lusts back to God.

On the other hand, Rebbe Aharon's 'easy' way to return to God is liable to create unstable returnees. These people could possibly fall once again and be drawn back to the pleasures of the outer husks. After all, they were not 'cured' of their addiction to pleasure, but simply exchanged physical pleasure for spiritual pleasure. These people must always be careful to feel the pleasure in holiness. If not, they will once again be drawn to unholy pleasures. This is similar to the people that Abraham and Sarah converted in Haran with their lovingkindness. These people 'disappeared' after Abraham and Sarah passed on, and apparently fell back into their old ways.

We need a *tzaddik* in our generation who unifies the ability to cause people to return to God out of pleasure with the *tzaddik* who has the ability to cause people to return to God by bringing them out of their false beliefs. The pleasure-based people need a *tzaddik* like Rebbe Aharon, while the people with the heretical beliefs need a *tzaddik* like the Alter Rebbe of Lubavitch, who had the ability to address false thoughts and beliefs and replace them with the truth.

On a deeper level, just as there is physical lust, there is also lust of the intellect, which is—in addition to its concomitant pride problem—the source of heresy. A person who is able to satiate intellectual lust with holiness and service of God (and override the arrogant, showing them that he is infinitely smarter than them) can bring heretics back to God. Today, we need both types of *tzaddikim*. If we merit, these two personas will unite in one persona—the Mashiach!

Rebbe Menachem Mendel of Vitebsk: To Set Sail on a Rickety Boat

Rebbe Menachem Mendel of Vitebsk was one of the great disciples of the Maggid of Mezritch. He was born to his father, Rebbe Moshe, who was a disciple of the Ba'al Shem Tov. He was orphaned at an early age and grew up in the home of the Rav the Maggid of Mezritch. The Maggid even took him with him when he would travel to the Ba'al Shem Tov. When the Rav the Maggid passed away and as per his will, Rebbe Menachem Mendel became the leader of the *chassidim* in White Russia and Lithuania. In an attempt to calm the rift and accusations against Chassidut within the Jewish communities, Rebbe Menachem Mendel of Vitebsk traveled together with the Alter Rebbe in order to meet the Vilna Gaon. The Vilna Gaon, however, pressured by his family, evaded the meeting and exited the city until Rebbe Menachem Mendel and the Alter Rebbe departed the city, as well.

In 5537 (1777), Rebbe Menachem Mendel made *aliyah* together with 300 of his *chassidim*. This was a very significant number of people to make *aliyah* as a group in that era. He first settled in Peki'in, then moved to Tzfat and finally to Tiberias, where his congregation settled.

Rebbe Menachem Mendel conducted himself and his court in a royal manner on an external level. Rebbe Yaakov Yosef of Polna'ah said that Rebbe Menachem Mendel conceals his deep lowliness specifically in what could be misinterpreted as grandeur. Rebbe Menachem Mendel would sign his letters with the subscript, "the truly lowly". Despite his youth, the disciples of the Ba'al Shem Tov admired him and Rebbe Pinchas of Kuritz even called him "the king of Israel."

Rebbe Menachem Mendel died on the first of Iyar, 5548 (1788) and was buried in the ancient cemetery of Tiberias, in the section of the students of the Ba'al Shem Tov. His student, Rebbe Elazar Zusman, collected his Torah teachings into the book, *"Pri Ha'aretz."*

To Continue the Ways of the *Tzaddikim* of the Land of Israel

From many stories about Rebbe Menachem Mendel, we can learn the proper path of the true *tzaddikim* regarding the establishment of the Jewish community in the Land of Israel. In the following story, we will also learn why it is so important:

When Rebbe Menachem Mendel and his followers reached Istanbul, on their way to the Land of Israel, they went to the port to choose a boat for the last leg of their journey. There were new, strong and safe boats at the port, but surprisingly, Rebbe Menachem Mendel chose an old, rickety boat anchored at the side of the port. Rebbe Menachem Mendel's decision also had to stand up to the test of a great storm that descended upon the travelers on the sea. The boat almost broke apart and Rebbe Mendel's special prayer that miraculously quieted the sea is the topic for another story. Why did the Rebbe choose this particular rickety boat? He sensed with his *ruach hakodesh* (Divine inspiration) that a spirit of holiness dwelled on the old boat. Later, they learned that approximately forty years earlier, Rabbi Elazar Rokeach, author of *"Ma'aseh Rokeach,"* had made *aliyah* with that boat.

One year after he was appointed Chief Rabbi of the important congregation of Amsterdam, Rebbe Elazar Rokeach, at the age of about 50, left his position and made *aliyah* to the Land of Israel with a messianic goal. Similar to the *aliyah* attempt of the Ba'al Shem Tov, who saw that if he would meet the holy Or Hachaim in Israel, they would be able to bring the redemption (the Ba'al Shem Tov did not manage to reach the shores of Israel), so Rebbi Elazar Rokeach hoped to bring the redemption by meeting one of the *tzaddikim* of the Land of Israel at that time—Rebbe Nachman of Horodonka. Rebbi Nachman of Horodonka was the grandfather of Rebbe Nachman of Breslev, who was named after him. He is also buried in the section of the disciples of the Ba'al Shem Tov in Tiberias. Ultimately (and as the Ba'al Shem Tov himself foresaw), Rebbi Elazar passed away within the year of his arrival in Israel, and never did meet Rebbe Nachman of Horodonka, who was overseas during that time.

Rebbe Menachem Mendel of Vitebsk, who also made *aliyah* with a messianic consciousness, preferred to travel with his hundreds of followers on a physically rickety but spiritually safe boat, as he saw that a spirit of holiness of a special *tzaddik* of the previous generation who had made *aliyah*, dwelled upon it.

This is an important lesson for our generation: Those who have merited that their mission in life is in the Land of Israel, building and developing it with the purpose of hastening the true and complete redemption (establishing the Kingdom of Israel in the path of the Torah in the Land of Israel, until the fulfillment of all the goals of the redemption in the Land) should identify with the *tzaddikim* who preceded them in this task, even if they must employ self-sacrifice. Even if it seems that there are newer, safer ways that will have more chance of success, we must continue in the boat of the *tzaddikim* of previous generations and identify with them. We must adopt their love of the Land of Israel, which was part of their complete cleaving to the ways of holiness, and their aspiration for the true and complete redemption. It is specifically with this rickety boat that we will reach our destination, with God's help.

Financial Independence in the Land of Israel

There are another two stories connected to the same point:

> "I heard from the Admor, (Our teacher, master, and rabbi) author of the *Birkat Avraham:* In the beginning, when Rebbe Mendele arrived in the Land of Israel, he settled in Peki'in. His plan was for the group to work the land for half a day and study Torah for half a day. The *ba'al davar* (evil force) came to him and told him that if he would not leave Peki'in, he would be leaving the world entirely. The *ba'al davar* threatened to focus strictly upon him. With no option to remain there, Rebbe Menachem Mendel left Peki'in. If he had remained there, it would have been possible for him to change the Heavens so that the abundance distributed to the entire world would come specifically from the Land of Israel. The *ba'al davar* did not agree to this." (*Vayehi Or*, page 120)

Before his *aliyah*, Rebbe Menachem Mendel founded the *Kollel Riessin* (and appointed the Alter Rebbe to head the Kollel) in order to attend to the financial needs of his followers who would be making *aliyah* with him. One time, the messenger who was to bring the funds raised overseas for the community in Tiberias was delayed, and starvation set in. When his followers complained to Rebbe Menachem Mendel, he replied, "Of course you are hungry. But why think about it all day? Do as I do: In the morning, I am hungry for about a quarter of an hour, which is the time that I am accustomed to eating breakfast. After that, I continue with my day. The same is true of the other meals. When you have food, you do not eat all day. And when there is no food, it is enough to be hungry at mealtime."

The words of the Rebbe sounded to them like an attempt to cheer them up, which did not fit their mood, and they continued to complain. Then the Rebbe said that he sees with his *ruach hakodesh* that the messenger is already nearby and that they can borrow money to buy food on credit. Later, Rebbe Menachem Mendel sorrowfully pointed out that if they had listened to his advice and held out for just a short time more, they would have absolved themselves of their dependence on funds from overseas and the community would have enjoyed financial independence.

These are deep and significant stories that are relevant to the time period in which we are involved with the independence of the Jewish community in the Land of Israel. The *tzaddikim* of the previous generations desired to achieve financial independence for the God-fearing Jewish community in the Land of Israel. (Here we can also highlight the response of the *Avnei*

Nezer, who says that the *mitzvah* of settlement of the Land of Israel is fulfilled only when one makes his living from it. The author of the *"Lev Ha'ivri"*, Rabbi Akiva Yosef Schlesinger, who passed away on the first of Iyar, as well, also strived in speech and action to establish agricultural settlements in the Land of Israel—for the financial independence of the Jewish community in Israel).

"The Land of Israel is acquired through hardship." In order to achieve true independence, we must safeguard our pure faith, expanded consciousness and focus our needs on what is truly necessary. In light of the previous story, we can say that in order to achieve pure Jewish independence, we sometimes have to forgo comfortable, safe and plush options and cling to the Land, while withstanding trials and making do with little. This is the way of the true *tzaddikim* who aspire to pure Jewish independence and Fear of Heaven.

REBBE MENACHEM MENDEL OF VITEBSK: THE TRULY LOWLY

Truly Lowly

Rebbe Menachem Mendel would sign all of his letters with the words, "the truly lowly, Menachem Mendel." What does this title mean? The example for this signature must have been King David, who danced before the Ark of the Covenant. When his wife, Michal told him that he was conducting himself in a decidedly unroyal manner, he answered her, "And I will make merry before God … and I will be lowly in my eyes."[1]

Lowliness can be an extremely poor characteristic, if a person does not respect himself-the Divine image in him-and allows himself to act like an animal. But lowliness can also be the best of traits. A lowly spirit goes together with humility and the sages guide us, "Be very, very lowly of spirit."

The essence of lowliness is when a person feels that he is very low, like a completely empty vessel that has nothing to claim as its own. This is not a license to be stupid. We must know and recognize our strong points and talents. It is important, however, to internalize that all our good points (and we

---

1. Samuel II, 6:22.

do have them) are a free gift from God in His abundant mercy and kindness. It is a gift from God with which we can fill our empty vessels.

In the words of Rebbe Menachem Mendel:

The main principle and root of all is that a person does not have the ability himself to perform an act … of mitzvot and good deeds and to cling to God's ways—only through the blessed Creator…

Rebbe Menachem Mendel and other chassidic masters taught that there is a special connection between positive lowliness and the Land of Israel. "Be very, very low of spirit" parallels the verse, "The Land is very, very good."[2] The truly lowly person has the tools to recognize the holiness of the Land of Israel and to live in it appropriately. In the Land of Israel, when we are dealing with the practical aspects of life, we must be very careful not to think that it is our own strength and talent that has brought us success. We must remember at all times that everything is from God. Thus, from the leader of the first "mass *aliyah*" in modern times, we learn the correct perspective of a true Jewish pioneer in the Land of Israel.

Fittingly, Rebbe Menachem Mendel chose to settle in Tiberias after unsuccessful attempts to settle in Tzfat and Peki'in. Tiberias is one of the lowest cities in the Land of Israel (second only to Jericho) and we can see it as representing the trait of lowliness; Tiberias is connected to the *sefirah* of acknowledgment (*hod*), about which it is said that it descends to what the Book of Formation calls, "the extreme depth," עומק תחת). The sages also say that Tiberias was the last place in which the *Sanhedrin* was active and that it will be reinstituted there in the future. Perhaps it was Rebbe Menachem Mendel who blazed the trail for the Sanhedrin…

---

2.   Numbers 14:7.

Rebbe Menachem Mendel of Vitebsk: Prayers Hovering Over the Kinneret

One time, before the beginning of the Friday pre-Shabbat *Mincha* prayers, Rebbe Menachem Mendel entered the synagogue but did not begin to pray. The entire congregation waited for him to begin, but Rebbe Menachem Mendel just stood and looked out the window at the Sea of Galilee (Kinneret) just below. He continued to look at the Kinneret, deep in contemplation. The sun set, night descended, and the congregation had not yet prayed the afternoon prayers. Suddenly Rebbe Menachem Mendel seemed to return to himself, smiled and began the prayers.

After the services, his students asked him what had transpired. He explained that all the prayers of the Jews of the Diaspora have to ascend on Shabbat eve, and they come to the Kinneret, hover over it and then ascend. "I looked at the Kinneret, at all the prayers hovering above it, and saw that they were not ascending. I understood that the Diaspora prayers were not ascending because some of the people there (referring to the *chassidim* connected to him) were not giving enough charity to help the poor in the Land of

Israel." Rebbe Menachem Mendel's deep contemplation was apparently effective, so that those people in the Diaspora decided to give generously for Israel's poor, which released the prayers and they ascended.

* * *

Charity in general, and charity for the Land of Israel in particular, is a very important matter in Chassidut. Most of the letters from the Alter Rebbe of Lubavitch that appear in the Tanya revolve around this theme. Why did the *tzaddik* have to wait so long for the prayers to ascend? Perhaps because the most auspicious time for giving charity is before lighting the Shabbat candles. In Europe, Shabbat begins late, and when the *chassidim* there were aroused to give charity, it was already quite late on the shores of the Kinneret.

Shabbat in the dimension of time (*shanah*) is parallel to the Land of Israel in the dimension of space (*olam*) and to the woman in the dimension of souls (*nefesh*). As such, it is very fitting to give charity for the Land of Israel before the woman of the house lights the Shabbat candles. The giving of the charity precipitates the ascent of the prayers, which are also relevant to the Shabbat. We can add another Shabbat to this beautiful tapestry: the Kinneret itself. *Pirkei D'erabbi Eliezer* lists seven seas surrounding the Land of Israel. The seventh sea, parallel to the seventh day, the Shabbat, is the Sea of Galilee, the Kinneret.

It is written that all the prayers ascend specifically from the Cave of Machpelah, the burial place of the Patriarchs and Matriarchs in Hebron. Apparently, there are two dimensions to the ascent of the prayers. The letters of the prayers and their intentions, their simple meaning and their soul. The revealed dimension ascends through Hebron (which in the

Zohar alludes to the connection to the natural elements and the letters of prayer) while the concealed dimension ascends from the Kinneret.

The concealed dimension of the prayers is very relevant to charity. When Rebbe Menachem Mendel saw that the prayers of the Diaspora had not ascended, he understood that the problem was in the realm of charity. He perceived that it was upon him to rectify the situation and to bring the prayers up to God. When a *tzaddik* is quintessentially lowly, like King David, he can uplift the entire reality to God. In the words of the Alter Rebbe of Lubavitch, "In order to lift a building, it must be grasped from below." In other words, when a *tzaddik* sees in everything in the world the point where it ascends to God, he can transform it into something truly lofty.

Rabbi Naftali Tzvi of Ropschitz: Messianic Holy Humor and the Intercepted Midnight Prayer

Rabbi Naftali Tzvi Horowitz of Ropshitz (Ropczyce) was born on the holiday of Shavuot in 5620 (1760)–the very day that the Ba'al Shem Tov passed away. Rabbi Naftali's father was Rabbi Menachem Mendel and his mother was Baila, the daughter of Rebbe Itzikel of Hamburg, under whose tutelage Rabbi Naftali learned Torah when he was young. Rabbi Naftali then studied under Rebbe Elimelech of Lizhensk. After Rebbe Elimelech's passing, he learned Torah from his student, the *Chozeh* Seer of Lublin and also studied under the Maggid of Kozhnitz and Rebbe Menachem Mendel of Rimanov. He was a rabbi in Ropschitz and additional cities, and after the passing of his rabbis, Rabbi Naftali became a chassidic Rebbe.

Rebbe Naftali was known (to be smart, endowed with a sharp wit. On his tombstone, it is written that he was "unique in his generation in Divine wisdom." He would dress his wisdom in humor and clever sayings. Among his disciples were Rebbe Chaim of Tzanz, Rebbe Shalom of Kaminkah, Rebbe Hanoch Henich of Alesk, Rebbe Yosef Baba'd, author of the *'Minchat Chinuch'* and more. He authored the books, *'Zera Kodesh'* and *'Ayala Shluchah.'* Rebbe Naftali passed away in Lantzut on 11 Iyar 5687 (1827) and was buried there.

The Royal Jester

Once, when Rebbe Naftali was studying in Lublin with his Rebbe, the *Chozeh* of Lublin, he heard two people arguing loudly in one of the adjacent homes. Two fathers-in-law to-be were quarreling about who was going to pay for the *badchan*, the wedding jester, a customary feature of weddings at that time. (In Hebrew, the root of *badach*/humor shares the same letters as Chabad.) Rebbe Naftali entered the home and turned to the two: "I don't like hearing such loud arguments, so I will come to the wedding and be the *badchan* for free." The two fathers happily accepted his offer and good cheer was restored.

Rebbe Naftali, as he had promised, went to the wedding a few days later, stood up on a table, and regaled the guests with humorous stories and wit. A good *badchan* can talk non-stop. Rebbe Naftali talked and talked and the guests laughed and laughed.

The *Chozeh* did not know about this, but when he arose at night to say the *Tikkun Chatzot* (midnight prayers and lamentations on the exile) he felt that something was not in order. The words just wouldn't come out of his mouth. Something was preventing him from saying *Tikkun Chatzot*!

The *Chozeh* called his assistant and asked him to check if something unusual was going on in the town. The assistant went out to search. He reached the wedding hall and saw the sight. He returned to the *Chozeh* and told him what he saw: There is a wedding at the other end of town, Rebbe Naftali is entertaining the guests with humor and everybody is laughing. The Seer understood that in Heaven, as well, there was much joy and laughter in the air, and with all the laughter in Heaven, he could not cry for *Tikkun Chatzot*.

The *Chozeh* decided that if he could not say *Tikkun Chatzot*, he would also go to hear his student's humor. The *Chozeh* hid outside the window of the wedding hall and listened to Rebbe Naftali for a long time, enjoying the Divine wisdom in every joke and play on words—truly secrets of secrets of the Torah.

Rebbe Naftali continued to delight the audience, while the *Chozeh* listened outside, until somebody told him that his Rebbe was outside, listening to his words. Rebbe Naftali immediately descended from the table and went outside to ask his Rebbe for forgiveness for speaking in his presence—and telling jokes, at that!

'There is no reason to apologize,' said the Rebbe, asking Rebbe Naftali to continue with his humorous act, because he was enjoying the presentation.

Rebbe Naftali felt that it was an *eit-ratzon*, a time of good will, and replied with holy boldness that he would be willing to continue on the condition that the Rebbe would agree to dance the *mitzvah-tantz* with the bride at the end of the wedding. (Until this very day, some of the chassidic courts have retained the custom that at the end of the wedding, the *tzaddik* dances before the bride, while both of them hold opposite ends of a long *gartel* or cord).

"My purpose at this wedding is to bring joy to the people and to draw holiness down to the wedding through humor (specifically through the power of the holiness of the humor)," said Rebbe Naftali to the *Chozeh* of Lublin. "I also request of the Rebbe, if he wants me to continue, that he will please dance with the bride." The *Chozeh*, who wanted to continue hearing the words of his disciple, agreed to the 'deal.' The story goes that one of the *tzaddikim* of the generation (whose name we do not know) was born from the union of this newly married couple.

Thus, Rebbe Naftali's *ruach hakodesh* to volunteer to be the *badchan* at the wedding, with the excuse of stopping the argument, ultimately brought the Seer of Lublin himself to come to the wedding and dance with the bride. And in the merit of the holy humor and the Rebbe's dance, one of the *tzaddikim* of the generation was born to the couple.

* * *

Holy Folly to Defeat the Impure Husk

There are many things that we can learn from this story, but the main point is the power of the *tzaddik*, Rebbe Naftali, to draw down the loftiest wisdom, dressed in worldly matters—and by doing so, to bring the Mashiach. This is the way of all the disciples of the Ba'al Shem Tov—each *tzaddik* with his unique path. Rebbe Naftali, however, excelled at this more than all the others. Humor is even part of his name. Chassidut explains that Naftali is made up of two words *"nofet li"*, which means, "sweetness to me," nectar and sweetness. Moreover, the month that corresponds to the tribe of Naftali is the month of Adar, which is the month that corresponds to the sense of laughter. (A gematria that adds potency to this thought: **Naftali Tzvi** equals **Purim Purim**. (פורים פורים), meaning that the average value of Rebbe Naftali's two names is Purim—the apex of laughter Drawing Godliness down to this world—to the point that it produces holy laughter—hastens the coming of the Mashiach.

Good and bad are in constant conflict in this world. Everything on the side of holiness has its opposite on the side of impurity. We learn of three levels of evil from the first verse in Psalms: "Happy is the man who did not walk with the counsel of the wicked, and in the way of sinners he did not stand, and in the gathering of scoffers he did not sit." It is written that the "counsel of the wicked" is the impure husk that corresponds to the "2000 years of void," first two-thousand years of history described by the sages as "chaos"; "the way of sinners" is the impure husk corresponding to the second two-thousand years, described as "Torah"; and the "gathering of scoffers" is the impure husk that corresponds to the final two-thousand years, described as, "the days of Mashiach." The main battle that we have today, on the eve of the Mashiach's arrival, is with the "gathering of scoffers," the worst impure husk. (The sages explained that the three stages of the verse describe three stages of deterioration).

How do we defeat the scoffers, the laughter of the impure husk? In his chassidic treatise, *"Bati Legani,"* the Rebbe Rayatz says that in order to defeat the impure husk that blocks the arrival of Mashiach, what is needed is "holy folly," —a holy *badchan*. To stand against the "gathering of scoffers," we need holy jesters like Rebbe Naftali and the Schpoler Zaydeh, who defeated the Cossack at his best game, as is related in the famous *niggun, "Hop Cossack."* To face off against the games of the impure husk, the "gathering of scoffers," we need wise people who know how to defeat the impure husk at its own game and on its own turf.

It is written that each of the Twelve Tribes, in the order they appear when the princes of each tribe are mentioned, corresponds to five hundred years of world history. Naftali is the last tribe toin this orderreckoning. Thus, the 500 years beginning with 5500 (1740 CE)—the year the Ba'al Shem Tov was 42, six years after he had revealed himself publicly—and extending to the end of the sixth millennium, all corresponds to Naftali who rectifies through laughter and holy humor. One can tell the secrets of secrets even within jokes. This is the holy, messianic humor of sharp-witted *tzaddikim* like Rebbe Naftali.

Rabbi Shimon Bar Yochai: Falling in Love with the Purifying Tzaddik

Rabbi Yitzchak David Grossman from Migdal Ha'emek received his guest from a nearby kibbutz warmly. The guest began to cry, relating that his son was about to marry a non-Jewish woman. "Even though we are not orthodox," he told the Rabbi, "I am still very upset. Can you speak to my son? Perhaps you can convince him to cancel his engagement."

Rabbi Grossman invited the young man to his home. He spoke with him at length and attempted to influence him, but to no avail. Rabbi Grossman then suggested a meeting between the son and the Rebbe of Lelov.

The son went to see the Rebbe of Lelov, who spoke with him about all sorts of topics, all completely unassociated with his marriage plans. After two and a half hours of conversation, the Rebbe said, "It was very pleasant to speak with you. May you be successful."

The young man returned home and told his father about his special meeting with the Rebbe. "Didn't the Rebbe speak to you about your marriage plans?" asked the confused father.

"No," the son answered. "Not one word."

The upset father phoned Rabbi Grossman. "My son sat with your Rebbe for two and a half hours, and the rabbi did not say a word to him about his upcoming marriage!" he angrily told him.

Rabbi Grossman immediately phoned the Rebbe of Lelov and told him that the father did not understand the purpose of his meeting with his son.

"Ask the father if his son enjoyed the conversation," the Rebbe of Lelov answered.

"The father told me that his son said that you are the most interesting person he has ever met," Rabbi Grossman said.

"If he fell in love with me," the Rebbe responded, "he will stop loving the non-Jewish woman."

A few days later, the son broke off the engagement.

Purifying Immersion

How can we overcome our evil inclination? How can we rid ourselves of all sorts of foreign thoughts and improper desires? This story teaches us that the main remedy for all problems is to "fall in love" with a *tzaddik* (a consummately righteous person). This is particularly true of the main *tzaddik* of the generation, who has nullified himself to God to the point where he can testify about himself "I am nothing more than a symbol"—a representative of God on this earth, as Rabbi Shimon Bar Yochai said about himself. Falling in love with Rashbi (Rabbi Shimon Bar Yochai) is as purifying as immersion in a *mikveh*.

When we fall in love with the consummate *tzaddik,* immersing ourselves in him, it is as if we are immersing ourselves in God, as Rabbi Akiva said, "God is the *mikveh* of Israel." About the unique wording in Exodus (23:17), "to see the face of the Master, Havayah," the Zohar asks, to what the words "the face of" refer. It answers that this is an allusion to Rabbi Shimon Bar Yochai." The connection to the consummate *tzaddik,* who is completely nullified to God and reflects Him, purifies those who connect to him.

Falling in love with a *tzaddik* helps a person to resolve his evil desires. his is what the Rebbe of Lelov said in our story, "If he falls in love with me, he will stop loving the non-Jewish woman."

This is similar to the teaching of the Alter Rebbe, the "Rabbi Shimon Bar Yochai" of Chassidut, who taught that love of God is a desire like all other desires. In order to merit this desire, however, one must rid himself of all the other desires in the world. This teaching of the Alter Rebbe makes achieving the proper love of God contingent upon nullifying all other improper loves. In our story, however, the process is reversed: by achieving the proper love of the *tzaddik,* the other, improper loves are spontaneously nullified.

This is the reason why hundreds of thousands of Jews throng to the burial place of Rabbi Shimon Bar Yochai on Lag Ba'omer. They connect to him with love. In the merit of that love, they rid themselves of their improper desires and merit the revelation of Mashiach.

Rabbi Mordechai of Chernobyl: Addicted to Money?

Rebbe Mordechai Twersky of Chernobyl was the son of Rebbe Menachem Nachum of Chernobyl. While his illustrious father lived in poverty, Rebbe Mordechai served God with great wealth. He even demanded large sums of money from his wealthy *chassidim*. Rebbe Mordechai had 8 sons, all of whom became chassidic rebbes. He passed away on 20 Iyar, 5597 (1837) and was buried in Anatevka, Ukraine.

Rebbe Mordechai had a special Chanukah custom. Every year, one of his wealthy *chassidim* would invite him to his home to light the Chanukah candles—a privilege for which Rebbe Mordechai would charge a grand sum of money.

One of Rebbe Mordechai's wealthy *chassidim* was as stingy as he was rich. He never invited Rebbe Mordechai to light the Chanukah candles at his home. He didn't want to pay the sum that the Rebbe would require of him and he also didn't want to deal with the mess and possible damage to his fine home, which would be the sure result of the Rebbe's visit with all his *chassidim* in tow.

One Chanukah, Rebbe Mordechai came to this *chassid*'s town. The *chassid* tried to avoid his Rebbe, but ultimately, he met him. Of course, he had to reluctantly invite him to light the Chanukah candles at his home. To his great relief, Rebbe Mordechai told the *chassid* that the honor would cost him only one thousand rubles—significantly less than what he could have requested.

The *chassid* readily agreed and invited Rebbe Mordechai to join him in his carriage for the trip to his home. But when Rebbe Mordechai heard that the house was so far away that it required travel, he turned to his *chassid* and said, "This journey to your home was not included in the original price. If we have to travel, it will cost another thousand rubles." The *chassid* had no choice. The two climbed into the carriage, Rebbe Mordechai's entourage of *chassidim* followed, and they set out.

When they arrived at the *chassid*'s home, Rebbe Mordechai saw that two or three flights of stairs had to be climbed. "I didn't realize that you lived on a high floor," said Rebbe Mordechai. "Every step will cost another thousand rubles."

The dejected *chassid* ascended the steps with Rebbe Mordechai and his entire entourage of *chassidim*, counting together with them the tens of steps that led to his home. Just as the *chassid* feared, the happy group was not overly concerned with the immaculate order in the house. The frustrated *chassid* sat in his chair, watching the *chassidim* trampling his carpets with their muddy boots, thinking about the tens of thousands of rubles that he now owed the Rebbe. The Rebbe approached his *chassid* with a document and asked him to sign: "This says that you are transferring all of your assets to me," Rebbe Mordechai explained. The *chassid* signed with a barely audible sigh, Rebbe Mordechai proceeded to the candle-lighting and afterward asked the *chassid* to accompany him outside.

"You should know," Rebbe Mordechai said to the *chassid*, "that until now, all of your money and assets were impure. Money is impure when it is acquired in forbidden ways. It could be profiting from a business that does not keep the Shabbat, negotiations that are not in good-faith, profits from taking cheap labor instead of employing your fellow Jews and the like. The impure money in your possession was the cause of your great stinginess. When impure money is in our hands, it is very hard to detach from it and use it to perform acts of loving-kindness. Now that you have transferred all of your assets to me, they have been purified. I am returning it all to you, except for the first one thousand rubles. I hope that from now on, you will safeguard the purity of your money."

From that day on, the *chassid* was very meticulous about the purity of his business transactions and became a philanthropist.

* * *

This story teaches us that an impure source of money distorts our proper approach to our possessions and livelihood and causes stinginess. Impure money comes from forbidden profits (such as fraud, interest, working on Shabbat, etc.) or from improper considerations (such as not taking the opportunity to fulfill the commandment that, "your brother shall live with you," ensuring that Jews have work and, "buy from your colleague," as well as giving livelihood to enemies of the Jewish people instead of to our friends and allies). When the source of our money is impure, instead of understanding that the money that God gives us is a deposit that He has placed in our hands, enabling us to do good in this world, we can become addicted to it, see it as the ultimate purpose instead of a means to an end—and have a hard time parting with it.

This is how the fourth Lubavitcher Rebbe, the Rebbe Maharash, explained the teaching of the sages, "A commoner is prohibited from eating meat." The word "prohibited" can also mean "bound." The sages' saying then becomes, "A commoner is bound to eating meat," meaning that he is or will become addicted to it. From an addictive state, one cannot free the holy sparks which themselves are bound in the meat (or whatever else one is addicted to). Instead of the meat being on his plate, he is, so to speak, on the meat's plate.

In our story, as well, the stingy *chassid* was addicted and bound to the vast sums of money he had acquired through forbidden means. Instead of controlling his wealth and using it properly, his wealth controlled him.

A person's money is part of the lofty soul level of the *yechidah* (the singular one) that hovers around us. When our approach to money is defective, our lust for wealth is tantamount to idol worship. In order to purify the money, we have to reach a level of self-sacrifice depicted by the words, "with all your might." This level of self-sacrifice also comes from the soul level of *yechidah*, as the sages explained that, "with all of your might" means, "with all your money." (This also rectifies those people for whom, "money is dearer than their own bodies").

"There is no man who does not have his hour (*sha'ah*, which also means "turn toward"). When the proper time comes, the miser's heart opens—even against his will—and he becomes part of the fulfillment of the statement, "Open for Me an opening the size of the point of a needle (one thousand rubles) and I will open for you an opening the size of a large hall "(all the money he owns). It is specifically the power of the Rebbe and *tzaddik* to actualize, "And Joseph gathered all the money"—to gather all the fallen longings (*kisufim*, the same root as *kesef*, 'money'), rectify them and elevate them to God.

Rebbe Shlomkeh of Zvhil: Shifting to God's Gear

Rebbe Shlomo Goldman of Zvhil was the fourth Rebbe in the Zvhil dynasty, son after son all the way back to Rebbe Yechiel Michel of Zlotshov, the disciple of the Ba'al Shem Tov. Rebbe Shlomkeh (as he was affectionately called by his followers) was born to Rebbe Mordechai Goldman, the third Rebbe in the dynasty and the Rebbe of Zvhil (which today is in Ukraine). Even while his father was still alive, Rebbe Shlomo conducted himself as a Rebbe and received *kvitlach* (prayer requests) from *chassidim*. In 5685 (1925), Rebbe Shlomkeh fled the Communist regime to Poland, and from there he made *aliyah* to the Land of Israel, settling first in the Old City of Jerusalem and later, in the Beit Yisrael neighborhood of Jerusalem. Even though he attempted to conceal his greatness, he became known in Jerusalem as a righteous *tzaddik*. Rebbe Shlomkeh passed away on the 26th of Iyar 5705 (1945) and was buried on the Mount of Olives. His son, Rebbe Gedaliah Moshe became the next Rebbe.

Were you ever on your way to do something good—and then something else unexpectedly came up?

In his service of God, Rebbe Shlomkeh emphasized proper treatment of others: He taught his disciples to be sensitive not to insult or harm others, and to help them as much as possible—even if it came at their own expense in the material or spiritual realms. There are several stories regarding questions that Rebbe Shlomkeh was asked about special stringencies in *kashrut,* matzah on Pesach and more. Rebbe Shlomkeh would always adamantly answer that when a Jew will get to Heaven after his 120 years here on earth, they will not ask him how many personal stringencies he exacted upon himself. Instead, they will ask him how careful he was in respecting others and how much he guarded his tongue and his eyes.

Once in the Study Hall, Rebbe Shlomkeh was going from person to person, trying very hard to make change for a large bill. When asked why he was so engrossed in this task, Rebbe Shlomkeh explained that he saw a Jew enter the Study Hall and unsuccessfully attempt to make change—and he wanted to help him. Rebbe Shlomkeh added that at the very moment that the man had walked into the Study Hall, he had felt about himself that his "wisdom had taken dominance over his actions" and in order not to remain, God forbid, in that condition, he hurried to take action to help a fellow Jew.

Actions Greater than Wisdom

From this story, we learn two important principles: The first, sensitivity to others. For Rebbe Shlomkeh, when someone needs something, we must dedicate ourselves to helping him. The second thing we learn is that if we are scholarly—even in Torah matters, while unwilling to act to help someone else—even for just a moment—we are in the wrong place. Wisdom is important and necessary but its inner dimension is selflessness. Ultimately, our actions must be more predominant than our wisdom. (As the Lubavitcher Rebbe put it, "The main thing is action").

Prayer for Someone Else

As is the case with all the *tzaddikim*, many people in need of spiritual succor would come to Rebbe Shlomkeh to request his prayers. Similar to Rabbi Chaninah Ben Dosa, who, when his prayers would flow easily from his mouth, knew that they had been accepted in Heaven, Rebbe Shlomkeh also used this gauge to know if his prayers had effected a Heavenly response. Rebbe Shlomkeh would frequent the Western Wall, and if he was not home when people would come to request his advice and prayers, his family would suggest that they look for him at the Western Wall. When someone would approach him at the Western Wall with a prayer request, Rebbe Shlomkeh would say, "Let us pray together for this request. We will say Psalms—" and would specify which chapters of Psalms to say for that particular problem or issue. He would pray together with the person, until he would feel that his prayers were flowing easily from his mouth and that they had evoked a Heavenly response.

Wondrously Patient

Rebbe Shlomkeh would also pray for the ill, specifically at their bedsides. Even when he was old and weak, he would take the trouble to reach the bedside of the ill to pray for them there.

Once, when Rebbe Shlomkeh was already old, his granddaughter needed an urgent operation. Rebbe Shlomkeh planned to go to the hospital to pray at his granddaughter's bedside during the operation. With one foot out the door, he was greeted by a poor, unhappy Jew, who began to tell him all his troubles. He did not have a specific request of Rebbe Shlomkeh—he just wanted a listening ear. The poor man proceeded to enumerate his misfortunes in detail, while Rebbe Shlomkeh stood and listened with great patience. He was "wondrous at patience" (an expression of the Rebbe Rayatz in *Hemshech tav shin hei*). By the time the man left Rebbe Shlomkeh, the operation was over and there was no reason for him to go to the hospital. Rebbe Shlomkeh said that he hoped that the merit of his patience in listening to the man and the lovingkindness that he had mustered helped his granddaughter as much as the prayers that he wanted to pray—and even more.

* * *

Sometimes, a person is about to do something or go somewhere and then suddenly someone else needs help or something else comes up to divert him from his plan. In Hebrew, this is called a *sibah*, a cause, like a large wheel that sets smaller gears into motion. In this story, Rebbe Shlomkeh was living with the cause that God had set into motion for him and fulfilled the adage, "Nullify your will before His will." Rebbe Shlomkeh's will was a holy will. He wanted to go to pray for his granddaughter. When God's Divine Providence arranged a different scenario for him, Rebbe Shlomkeh immediately shifted gears, nullifying his own will and seamlessly shifting to God's will.

The source of the "causes," called *sibot* in Hebrew, is found in God's transcendent light, known as the *sovev* (which has the same root as *sibah*, "cause" in Hebrew). The source of the will for holiness in man's consciousness is in God's immanent light. When the causes from God's transcendent light manifest, they override, nullify or change our personal good will, sourced in God's immanent light.

So the next time you are about to embark on a good deed and someone or something needs your urgent and often frustrating attention, remember that this is an opportunity for you to connect to God's transcendent light and to draw even more holiness into the world than you had originally intended.

REBBE MENACHEM MENDEL OF VORKE: DRIVE THOSE HORSES

Rebbe Menachem Mendel Kalish of Vorke (Warka), whose day of passing is the 16th of Sivan, was the son of Rebbe Yitzchak of Vorke– the preeminent disciple of Rebbe Simcha Bunim of Parshischa (Przysucha). There was another great *tzaddik* in that generation, whom many considered the greatest *tzaddik* of the times: Rebbe Yisrael of Ruzhin. Rebbe Yisrael of Ruzhin was the only *tzaddik* that his contemporary, the third Lubavitcher Rebbe (known as the *Tzemach Tzedek*) referred to as holy–"the holy Ruzhiner." Rebbe Yisrael of Ruzhin devoted his life to bringing the Mashiach.

The *tzaddikim* of Poland used to meet often. Once, Rebbe Yitzchak of Vorke went to meet the Ruzhiner Rebbe, and brought his teenaged son, Rebbe Menachem Mendel, with him. Rebbe Yisrael of Ruzhin maintained a markedly royal court. He had a grand carriage upon which he would ride like a king. He ascended onto the carriage, inviting his guests to ascend after him. As they were ascending, Rebbe Yisrael announced, "Whoever does not know the secret of the Workings of the Chariot may not ascend onto the carriage."

The secret of the Workings of the Chariot is the deepest secret in the Torah. The sages teach us that there are two secrets, one deeper than the other;

together they are the secrets and the secret of secrets. The first secret is the Workings of Creation and the greater secret—the secret of secrets—is the Workings of the Chariot.

Rebbe Yitzchak of Vorke knew the secret and ascended unperturbed. But as soon as his son, the teenaged Menachem Mendel heard the words of Rebbe Yisrael of Ruzhin, he jumped into the driver's seat of the carriage, saying, "I don't know the Workings of the Chariot, but I do know how to drive horses!" And off they went. Menachem Mendel drove the carriage while the two *tzaddikim* in the back relaxed and enjoyed each other's Torah thoughts.

At a certain point, Rebbe Yisrael of Ruzhin turned to his colleague and asked, "How did you merit such a son? How did you merit to bring the soul of this son down into the world?"

"This son is a pure gift from Heaven, above and beyond any merit," Rebbe Yitzchak answered.

* * *

What can we learn from this story? Rebbe Menachem Mendel's modesty and humility elicited his statement that he does not know the secret of the Workings of the Chariot. But he does say that he knows how to drive the carriage.

The Lubavitcher Rebbe repeated many times that "the main thing is action." Rebbe Menachem Mendel is a great *tzaddik,* who also knows how to descend into reality, control the horses and drive the carriage. This is very special. To merit a son like that, a great *tzaddik* who is both modest, humble and strong—who jumps in and immediately begins driving the carriage—represents a form of messianic perfection.

There is nothing new about a person who is not learned in Torah knowing how to drive horses. But when a genuinely great *tzaddik*, modest and humble says, "I don't know the secret of the Workings of the Chariot, but I do know how to drive horses," and then jumps into the carriage and starts driving two great *tzaddikim*—he is expressing true messianic energy. This is also the energy that we need to build the Land of Israel. When the Jewish Nation returns to its Land, it has to be actively involved in reality —but it also has to be righteous. "And Your people are all *tzaddikim*, they will inherit the Land eternally."[1] This synthesis is very rare, but it is the destiny of our generation.

---

1.   Isaiah 60:21.

The Beit Aharon of Karlin: The Safest Minyan of All

Rebbe Aharon Perlow of Karlin-Stolin was the fourth Rebbe in the Karlin dynasty. He was the son of Rebbe Asher of Stolin (who grew up in the home of Rebbe Shlomo of Karlin, the disciple of the Great Rebbe Aharon of Karlin) and the grandson of the Great Rebbe Aharon of Karlin. After the passing of his father, he was appointed to lead his congregation in Karlin. Rebbe Aharon was very connected to the Land of Israel. He raised money for charity for Israel and supported his *chassidim* in Tiberias and Jerusalem. His book, *Beit Aharon,* includes the Torah teachings of his grandfather, his father and himself. It is a fundamental work of Karlin chassidic thought and one of the basic works in the chassidic library. Rebbe Aharon passed away on Motza'ei Shabbat, 17 Sivan 5632 (1872) on his way to his granddaughter's wedding. He is buried in Melinov, Ukraine. Rebbe Aharon's son, Rebbe Asher, succeeded him.

The *chassid* S.S.P told the following story. He heard it from Rabbi Yaakov Shemesh, who heard it from his mother, who heard it straight from his grandfather, who was the assistant of the holy *Beit Aharon* of Karlin and lived to be one hundred years old. The assistant related that he merited to reach an advanced age in the merit of the blessing of the holy Rebbe Aharon.

Rebbe Aharon never prayed without a quorum (*minyan*). Once, he had to have surgery and he was given general anesthesia. Before the surgery, Rebbe Aharon and his followers prayed the afternoon prayer. They agreed that they would pray the evening prayer after Rebbe Aharon would awaken from the anesthesia. They had ten men, necessary for the quorum, waiting for the Rebbe to wake up. The Rebbe, however, did not wake up on time, and eventually, the men prayed the evening prayer without him.

When the Rebbe woke up, he asked his assistant when they would be praying the evening prayer. The assistant exited the Rebbe's room and began to say *Kaddish* and *Barchu*, as if there was a quorum of men praying with him.

Some time later, after the Rebbe had recovered and was out for a stroll with his assistant, the assistant turned to him and said, "Rebbe, there is something weighing heavily upon me."

"What is bothering you?" asked Rebbe Aharon.

The assistant told the Rebbe what had transpired with the prayer. "May you live a long life!" Rebbe Aharon blessed him. "Danger to life overrides every other commandment. At the time, I would not have been able to bear the thought of not praying with a quorum."

* * *

Praying with a Quorum—the Service of Abraham

The Divine service of every *tzaddik* includes the three Patriarchs (who are representative of God's chariot). Rebbe Aharon excelled at the attribute of "truth for Jacob—" so much so, that his in-law, the holy Rebbe of Ruzhin, said that if Rebbe Aharon would know that the truth was buried eight cubits underground, he would dig with his bare hands in order to unearth a piece of it. Rebbe Aharon would also say, "When I go out into the street and return safely and see that all my limbs and organs are whole and healthy, I sing a song of praise to God." This is the attribute of Isaac, who fulfilled the directive to "live in the land" (Genesis 26:3) and was "imprisoned in his home" at the end of his days, when he sensed that his main focus should be on the inner service of God and that, "all the paths [outside] are considered dangerous." Our story above, however, expresses Rebbe Aharon's deep connection to Abraham—an elemental factor in the Divine service of a person named Aharon (after Aharon, the High Priest, who like Abraham is described as a man of lovingkindness).

Aharon the High Priest (*Avot* 1:12) "loved peace" (meaning that he loved the people) and "pursued peace" (meaning that he prayed for the people). The core of the service of prayer is love. Thus, "Abraham who loves Me" (Isaiah 41:8), our first patriarch, is the first to institute prayer—the morning prayer, as the sages learn from the verse, "And Abraham awakened early in the morning."[1] Abraham did not have a quorum of Jews with whom to pray. But the potential for all the public prayers of all Israel is in him.

The inner dimension of public prayer is to approach prayer with the love of God, which reaches its ultimate goal when we

---

1. Genesis 22:3.

love that which the beloved loves." This means to love all of God's beloved children. This is why, prior to prayer, we say, "I accept upon myself the positive commandment, "Love your fellow as your self" (Leviticus 19:18). We do so in order to connect with the entire congregation and all the souls of Israel on an authentic, inner plane. In the merit of that connection, the prayer (which also serves as a sacrifice) is like a complete sacrifice, reflecting the completeness of all the souls (not missing any limb or organ, God forbid). This is the secret of God's directive to Abraham, "Walk before Me and be complete."[2]

The Devotion of the Assistant

When a *tzaddik* (every Jew is a *tzaddik,* as the prophet says, "And Your people are all *tzaddikim*"; Isaiah 60:21) sacrifices himself for a *mitzvah* or a custom, he merits special heavenly help to be able to fulfill it. In this story, the self-sacrifice is expressed—beyond the daily prayer in a quorum—by the fact that prayer in a quorum touches upon the very essence of Rebbe Aharon's soul and is a matter of life and death for him. Unexpectedly, the heavenly help in this story comes in the form of, "a sin so that someone else can merit." The assistant sinned by creating a false impression in order to merit his Rebbe. The Rebbe is an all-inclusive soul and his merit of keeping his thrice-daily custom of praying in a quorum is also the personal merit of everyone who is truly connected to him. The assistant's decision to pretend that there was a quorum for the Rebbe was an example of, "a sin for the sake of Heaven is greater than a good deed not for the sake of Heaven" (*Nazir* 23b and *Horayot* 10b),

---

2.   Genesis 17:1.

which the sages learn from the verse "Know Him in all your ways,"[3]—the mode in which Abraham conducted himself.

Ultimately, it turns out retroactively that the assistant's decision also conformed to Jewish law (for danger to life overrides all commandments of the Torah), as we have seen in many other instances of rabbinical directives that apply to particular emergency situations (*hora'at sha'ah*). This is also typical of Aharon, who would alter the truth a bit in order to promote peace. By doing so and not telling the harsh truth and encouraging strife, he was actually consistent with the inner dimension of truth, which, in his merit, can then appear in external reality, as well.

In the merit of the assistant's loving devotion to the attribute of Abraham, he merited the blessing of Abraham, "And Abraham was old, coming of days."[4]

---

3.   Proverbs 3:6.
4.   Genesis 24:1.

REBBE YAAKOV YITZCHAK OF BLENDOV: LOVESICK FOR THE REDEMPTION

Rebbe Yaakov Yitzchak Shapira of Blendov was born to his father, Rebbe Chaim Meir Yechiel, the grandson of the Maggid of Kozhnitz, and his mother, who was the granddaughter of Rebbe Elimelech of Lizhensk. His father named him after the "Holy Jew" and said that all his Torah teachings were for his son, Yaakov Yitzchak. Rebbe Yaakov Yitzchak was known for his intense enthusiasm in the service of God and his strong stance on matters brought before him, in which he favored no one, regardless of their station. He was extremely modest and avoided any type of honor. He passed away on the 24th of Sivan, 5642 (1882) and was laid to rest in Warsaw. Over twenty thousand people participated in his funeral. After his passing, all five of his sons became chassidic Rebbes. Rebbe Yaakov Yitzchak's Torah teachings were compiled in the book, *Emet L'Yaakov.*

Rebbe Zelig Elazar of Kozhnitz, the son of Rebbe Yaakov Yitzchak of Blendov related that on the eve of Passover in the year 5600 (1840), his father heard comments from his grandfather, Rebbe Chaim Meir Yechiel, alluding to the coming of Mashiach very soon. This was further supported by teachings in the Zohar. Rebbe Yaakov Yitzchak stated that he did not feel capable or ready to receive the Mashiach. He became so worried that he fell ill with a high fever

until the holiday of Shavuot, after which he returned
to good health, with God's help.

* * *

There are 49 days between Passover and Shavuot, the numerical
value of חולה, ill. A known teaching from Rebbe Abraham the
Angel, the son of the Maggid of Mezritch, and from additional
tzaddikim is that the days of the Counting of the Omer between
Passover and Shavuot are days of potential for the coming of
Mashiach. Feelings of not being worthy or prepared for the
coming of Mashiach can make one vulnerable to fear (חיל) and
trembling and eventually to illness (מחלה) during these days.
The root of all illness is in the emotion described in the Song of
Songs, "I am sick with love (for God)."

The majority of the days in which we count the Omer are
all the days of the month of Iyar. 'Iyar' (אייר) is an acronym
for "*Ani Hashem Rofecha*" (I am God, your Healer). Both the
illness and the remedy come in tandem during the days that
we count the omer. This is like the Mashiach, himself, who is
called "*bar naflah*" (a person who falls) because he falls and rises
every moment.

This story is particularly connected to the End of Days
alluded to in the Zohar regarding the year 5600 (1840), as per
the verse, "In the sixth hundredth year of the life of Noah…all
the fountains of the great deep burst open and the windows of
heaven were opened (Genesis 7:11). This allusion to the End
of Days pertains to the connection between the wisdom of the
Torah (the upper waters) and the wisdom of nature and science
(the lower waters), which began to flow with more intensity
during this year. The feeling that we are not succeeding in
properly unifying Torah and science—and that a gap between

them, which delays the redemption, has been created (distancing Jews from Torah observance)—creates illness, existential worry. This should energize us to take proper action to unify these waters, until we are restored to our good, redemptive health, with God's help.

The Lubavitcher Rebbe: Connecting with Thought

Rabbi Menachem Mendel Schneerson, the revered and beloved 7th Lubavitcher Rebbe, revolutionized world Jewry and influenced the entire world to draw closer to God. The Rebbe is the one individual more than any other singularly responsible for stirring the conscience and spiritual awakening of world Jewry. Born in Russia on 11 Nissan 5662 (1902), the Rebbe escaped Holocaust-torn Europe, joining his father-in-law, the 6th Lubavitcher Rebbe in NY. After his father-in-law's passing, the Rebbe continued his work, establishing a worldwide Chabad empire of loving kindness, outreach and Chassidut. His day of passing is on the 3rd of Tamuz.

After a number of years, Josh and his wife were finally blessed with their first child. Their joy knew no bounds. But just a few short minutes after the birth, a doctor entered the delivery room and sorrowfully announced to the parents that their baby had a serious eye condition, which would most likely render him blind. The only small chance that they had to prevent the blindness to a certain extent would be an operation—which was immediately scheduled for two days later. The crushed mother remained in the delivery room, while the father went to sit outside.

A Chabad *chassid,* an emissary of the Lubavitcher Rebbe, had set up a tefillin-donning stand near where Josh was sitting. It was a Friday. "Would you like to put on tefillin?" he asked Josh, who was Jewish but not connected.

"Just leave me alone," Josh replied. "I'm not into that."

The *chassid* saw that Josh was sad. "What's wrong?" he asked.

"Just leave me alone," Josh replied. But the *chassid* kept trying. After a few more questions, Josh told the *chassid* about his new baby.

"In a case like this, we have to immediately phone the Lubavitcher Rebbe and request his blessing," the *chassid* said.

Josh had never heard of the Rebbe and had no idea how to request a blessing, but the *chassid* was adamant.

"You know what?" Josh finally broke down. "You take care of it. Go home, call the Rebbe and ask for a blessing."

The *chassid* went home to place the long-distance call, but could not get through. He tried all day Friday but was unsuccessful. Finally, he returned to the hospital and told Josh that he had not managed to speak with the Rebbe's office to request a blessing.

This *chassid* was originally from Russia, during the era when there was no communication from behind the Iron Curtain. "Do you know what we *chassidim* used to do in Russia when we had a problem and could not communicate with the Rebbe?" he turned to Josh. "We discovered that we could communicate with him through our thoughts. We would simply think about the Rebbe in a very focused manner while requesting a blessing or advice—whatever we needed. It worked very well in Russia. So now, when we haven't managed to get our call through, let us both connect to the Rebbe in our thoughts, both of us, together. We will ask the Rebbe for a blessing for your baby."

If Josh hadn't been feeling so miserable, he would have laughed. But the *chassid* continued unperturbed. He removed a picture of the Rebbe from his pocket and showed it to Josh. "This is the Rebbe," he told him. Focus on his picture and ask him for his blessing and prayers to God for your baby."

"You do it," said Josh. The *chassid* did it, with Josh looking on.

Shabbat was approaching, and the *chassid* went home. On Sunday morning, he returned to the hospital and saw Josh—who was looking very happy. "This morning," Josh related, "just before the operation, the doctors came in to tell us that what they had diagnosed on Friday was wrong. There is just a small problem, and it is most likely that our baby will be able to see."

"The Rebbe's blessing worked!" said the *chassid* joyously.

Josh didn't think it had much to do with the Rebbe, but left it at that.

Two years passed. Josh and his family attended a business convention near New York.

Josh was friendly with one of the Orthodox Jews at the convention. "My son's *bar-mitzvah* is approaching," he told Josh. "I am flying to New York with my son for the day to get a dollar and blessing from the Lubavitcher Rebbe. (The Rebbe would give dollars for charity and blessings to thousands of Jews every Sunday). Why don't you join me?"

"No thanks," Josh answered.

"But there is nothing happening at the convention today," the friend said to Josh. "It's just a short flight, and we'll be back in plenty of time for the rest of the convention tomorrow."

Josh agreed and brought his wife and now two-year-old baby along.

In line, waiting for the dollar from the Rebbe, Josh asked his friend not to say anything to the Rebbe about him. He wanted to remain completely anonymous.

"No problem," his friend replied. "I will go first with my son, and then you can follow. I won't say a word about you."

The Rebbe showered many blessings upon the *bar-mitzvah* boy. Josh followed, with his son in his arms. The Rebbe did not say anything to him, beyond two words when handing him the dollar, "Blessing and success." But then, unexpectedly, the Rebbe looked at the child, moved his finger back and forth in front of his eyes, and when he saw that the child followed his finger, smiled.

Josh was totally shocked and eventually became a Chabad *chassid*.[1]

* * *

Connection to the Tzaddik in Thought, Speech and Action

This story shows us how we can connect to a *tzaddik* with the power of thought. Now, after the third of Tamuz, the main way to connect to the Rebbe is with our thoughts.

The soul has three garments: Thought, speech and action. We can communicate with thought. The main way to communicate is through speech. And we can also communicate through action. Communication through action can be accomplished by writing a letter. Everything that we write today—by email, for example—is communication through action.

The three garments of the soul parallel the three worlds of Action, Formation and Creation. The World of Creation parallels thought, the World of Formation parallels speech and the World of Action parallels action. These are different methods of communication.

Three Gardens of Eden

The Upper Garden of Eden is in the World of Creation. The Lower Garden of Eden is in the World of Formation and what is known as 'The Garden of Eden on Earth' is in the World of Action. This is where Adam and Eve were prior to their sin—in

---

1. This story was told by Rabbi Buket, who met Josh at the Rebbe's resting place. Josh told him the entire story, which happened over twenty years ago.

a place here in this world. Today, we cannot find the Garden of Eden on Earth. Spiritually, the Lower Garden of Eden is above the Garden of Eden on Earth.

When a person performs a *mitzvah*, it consists of thought, speech and action. There is the action itself, there is the intention, which is thought and there is the blessing said before performing the *mitzvah*, which is speech. With the power of his action, the person who performed the *mitzvah* reaches the Garden of Eden on Earth. With the power of his blessing, he reaches the Lower Garden of Eden and with the power of his intention, his soul connects to the World of Creation, the Upper Garden of Eden.

Connecting to the Rebbe through Thought

Any time that we connect to a *tzaddik*, we are in the Garden of Eden. There is nothing better than connecting to the Rebbe. Today, many people write letters to the Rebbe and get answers through the books of the Rebbe's letters to others. This is an example of communication through action, which parallels the Garden of Eden on Earth.

There is also communication with speech. When we go to the burial place of a *tzaddik*, we connect with him and can actually speak to him. This parallels the Lower Garden of Eden.

Now, after the third of Tamuz, the main place to seek the Rebbe and communicate with him is in the Upper Garden of Eden, with the power of our thought. This depends on our ability to picture the *tzaddik* in our minds and communicate with him. It is a special power that resonates with the third of Tamuz— allowing us to reach the Garden of Eden of the World of Creation.

Three Stories About the Lubavitcher Rebbe

Silent for One and Speaking for Another

Our first story took place in the period that the Rebbe—still called the Rama"sh (Rabbi Menachem Schneersohn)—was serving as the right-hand-man of his father-in-law, the previous Lubavitcher Rebbe, Rabbi Yosef Yitzchak Schneersohn:

In 5707 (1947) the Rebbe traveled to Paris to greet his mother, who had managed to leave Russia. He invited three of the Lubavitcher *chassidim* who were in Paris at the time—Rabbi Nachum Shemaryah Shashunkin, Rabbi Ben Tzion Shemtov, and Rabbi Zalman Sodkevitch (who told this story) to come to see him. Each of the three had personal issues to discuss with the Rebbe. The Rebbe first began speaking with Rabbi Shashunkin, while Rabbi Zalman felt an overwhelming urge to doze off. Afterward, the Rebbe turned to speak with him and suddenly, he was clear-headed and completely alert, while he noticed that the other two *chassidim* were sleeping. When it came time for the Rebbe to speak with Rabbi Shemtov, the other two fell soundly asleep…

* * *

This story wonderfully epitomizes the Ba'al Shem Tov's explanation of the secret of Chashmal: that a true *tzaddik* can be silent
(*chash*) for those people to whom his words are not directed
and simultaneously speak (*mal*) with others. In this story, we
see that even before the Rebbe officially became the Rebbe, he
was already empowered with the secret of *chashmal*.

From this we can also conclude that the Rebbe was also
empowered with the second explanation of the Ba'al Shem Tov
for the secret of *chashmal*—the secret of the process of submission, separation and sweetening (*chash-mal-mal*)—and to posit
that this is why the Rebbe invited these three *chassidim*, to parallel *chash-mal-mal*: To one of the *chassidim* the Rebbe spoke words
of submission (*chash*), to the second, words of separation (*mal*)
and to the third, words of sweetening (*mal*)—to each according to his own soul root and the rectification that he needed in
general, and in particular, at the time of their conversation.

The Rebbe and Those Who Come With Him

This story took place in the first year that the Rebbe had already
assumed the mantle of leadership after his father-in-law's
passing. At the time, he was still performing wedding ceremonies.

> An engaged couple asked the Rebbe to perform their
> wedding ceremony. The Rebbe asked the bride if
> she was planning to cover her hair with a wig. The
> bride answered that she was planning to cover her
> hair with a headscarf. Despite the Rebbe's words
> that a headscarf can sometimes slide back or even
> fall off the head so that it is preferable to wear a wig,
> the bride remained firm—and the Rebbe said that if
> that is the case, he could not perform the wedding

ceremony. On the morning of the wedding, the groom came to the Rebbe's headquarters at 770 and told the Rebbe that the bride had accepted upon herself to wear a wig and in light of her decision, they once again request the Rebbe to perform their wedding ceremony. The Rebbe answered that it was too late. "But the wedding is still hours away," the surprised groom wondered. "Certainly your intention is not for me alone to come, but rather that I will be accompanied by he who comes with me. And for that, it is already too late…," the Rebbe replied.

* * *

In this story, we see how the Rebbe saw himself. Clearly, the groom wanted the Rebbe's presence at the wedding. The groom was not consciously aware of, "that which comes with the Rebbe." Actually, this was a phrase the Rebbe often used to refer to his connection with his departed father-in-law, the Previous Rebbe. The Rebbe used this phrase in the first period following the passing of his father-in-law and explained once: "In truth, it matters not to whom he [the previous Rebbe] is connected himself. We are connected to him and for us, there is nothing higher than that." The Rebbe emphasized—particularly in the year before he accepted the mantle of leadership upon himself (5710, or 1950) and in the first year of his being a Rebbe—that he was nothing more than a connection to his father-in-law, the "the *Nassi* (leader) of our generation." He saw himself as nothing at all, and that he is mainly "that which comes with [him]." The Rebbe—unsuccessfully—tried to impress this upon his followers, the *chassidim*, while at the same time not surrendering his own assertiveness and firm approach on various issues, for example, on wearing a wig as a head-covering, a topic that came to be known as, "one of the Rebbe's issues."

The Rebbe's *Chassid*: With all Powers of the Soul

The third story took place many years later, after the Rebbe's unique leadership capabilities were already clear to all, through his *mitzvah* campaigns, (called *mivtzo'im*) the public struggles that he took upon himself, and his focus on the redemption and Mashiach, as we will see in the following story:

> Rabbi Chaim Hakohen Gutnick, o.b.m., former head of the Beit Din of Melbourne, once asked the Rebbe if he should change his British-style rabbinical hat to a regular Chabad-style hat so that he would look like a *chassid*. The Rebbe answered: True, one of the Chabad Rebbes expressed that he was jealous of the garments of the *chassidim* of Poland, but if they would show him a *chassid* from the previous generations, he would be able to immediately know if he was a *chassid* of the Alter Rebbe, the Mittler Rebbe or the *Tzemach Tzedek*. Not according to his apparel, but according to the matter to which he enthusiastically devotes himself (in Yiddish, *koch zich*).
>
> The Rebbe continued: My *chassidim* are enthusiastically devoted to three things: 1. *Mivtzo'im* (campaigns) that include the three pillars upon which the world stands. Implementing them strengthens the world. 2. Jewish pride (the Rebbe spoke at length about the "Who is a Jew?" issue, but on a simple level this also includes the struggle for the entire land

of Israel). 3. "To live Mashiach"—every thought, speech, and action are focused on "bringing the Days of Mashiach."

* * *

The three items that the Rebbe stated encompass all the levels of the *chassid*'s soul.

The *mivtzo'im* parallel the powers of implementation and action in the soul—the behavioral powers of the soul, associated with the *sefirot* of victory, acknowledgment, and foundation (*netzach, hod,* and *yesod*). The initiative for implementation comes from victory, which combined with submission to or acknowledgment of the Rebbe's instructions transforms every *chassid* into a pious individual, who is described as, "a foundation of the world"; it is the pious, the *tzaddikim,* who sustain reality, as in the Rebbe's words that the *mivtzo'im* strengthen the world's existence.

Jewish pride begins with an individual sense of personal lowliness, which is then complemented by the positive pride shared by the members of an elite military unit. In all, Jewish pride builds upon the faculties of the heart. The public struggles that the Rebbe took upon himself derived from the depths of his heart and touched upon areas that were especially dear to him. This is the level of the emotive powers of the soul, the sefirot of lovingkindness, might, and beauty (*chesed, gevurah,* and *tiferet*). In short, the boundless love of Israel stemming from Loving-kindness (on the right axis) brings about the firmness of Might (from the left axis) when steadfastness is needed in the struggles; the two are then balanced by the sefirah of beauty (of the middle axis).

The main innovation found in the Rebbe's teachings is that

the redemption and Mashiach are the essential points of the service of the Chabad intellect throughout the generations. The Rebbe revealed in a letter that consciousness of the redemption and Mashiach had accompanied him from his earliest years, when he began attending school, and even earlier. From that point on, he longed for the redemption and contemplated when it would come about, it would become possible to apply the verse, "I thank You, God, for being angry with me" to all the tribulations of the exile as an ultimate consolation. This Chabad consciousness focuses the *chassid* and permeates all his thoughts, speech and action with the ultimate purpose of Creation—the coming of Mashiach. This issue is related to the intellect and the intellectual sefirot in the soul: wisdom, under-standing, and knowledge *(chochmah, binah,* and *da'at).* Wisdom, which is described in the Zohar as a "penetrating point" turns the *chassid* into someone firmly permeated with the point of Mashiach and the redemption; the fire of understanding keeps his thoughts constantly brewing; knowledge focuses and con-centrates the mind on the issue.

The stories are from the book, Ma'aseh B'Rebbe, Rabbi A.D. Halperin, Sifriyat Kfar Chabad.

The Rebbe's Crown in the Merit of His Mother

The Lubavitcher Rebbe was very careful about honoring his mother, Rebbetzin Chanah Schneersohn. Whenever he would finish his daily visit with her, he would take leave with his face toward her, walking backward, so as not to turn his back on her. Once, a friend of the Rebbetzin's noticed the Rebbe's conduct, and said to Rebbetzin Chanah in amazement, "How beautiful how your son honors you!" The Rebbe's mother replied, "Since his Bar Mitzvah, I have not seen his back!"

* * *

"I Will Walk Before God"

Let us delve into not turning one's back. One of the collections of the early teachings from the Alter Rebbe is named *Et'halech* (אתהלך), which means, "I will walk." The name is taken from the verse opening the first teaching "I will walk before God in the lands of the living"[1] In that essay,[2] the Alter Rebbe explains that the word *et'halech* does not refer to walking directly to the destination, but is more like a to-and-fro movement—which, to use a Biblical reference from Ezekiel, is known as a run-and-return. One draws near and then backs off. This is the type of movement that governs the way in which we serve God. There are times when we draw closer to God. These are times of expanded consciousness, when we feel an ascent in our service. But there are also times when we retreat; times when our minds and consciousness feel contracted and distant from anything holy.

King David says, as the Alter Rebbe explains, that no matter what the condition of our *et'halech*, no matter how we are walking—both when we are drawing near and when we are backing away—we are always, "before God." When we draw near, we turn to face God. But even when we fall and back away, we continue to face God. Even when we are in a period of contracted consciousness, says the Alter Rebbe, when we have fallen and backed away, we still think about God.

This is the secret of honoring one's parents. The Rebbe was careful not to turn his back on his mother both when he was coming close and when he was backing away, his relationship with her remained face-to-face. He was still thinking about her and kept his eyes on her.

"With the Crown that His Mother Crowned Him"

We can assume that the Rebbe was meticulous about honoring both his parents, but if by Divine Providence this story is specifically about his mother, we can further explore this point.

---

1. Psalms 116:9.
2. *Ma'amarei Admor Hazaken, Et'halech Lozhnya*, p. 1.

It is known that before the *shidduch* (agreement to marry) between the Lubavitcher Rebbe and the Previous Lubavitcher Rebbe's daughter, Rebbetzin Chayah Mushka, was concluded, Rebbetzin Chanah hinted—and even more than that—that the *shidduch* was with the understanding that her son would be the previous Rebbe's successor. The previous Rebbe did not want to explicitly commit to that, so he said, "the *chassidim* are smart, they will certainly choose the appropriate person...." Rebbetzin Chanah understood this as an agreement with her request, and the *shidduch* was concluded.

If so, we can say that in great measure, it was the Rebbe's mother, Rebbetzin Chanah, who made sure to crown her son with the mantle of leadership (from her internal, essential understanding that he was truly the person worthy to be the leader of the Jewish people). We can also say that the Rebbe was so meticulous in his honor for her for this reason.

From this story, we see that in many aspects, it is the mother, more than the father, who takes care of the son's "crown." The mother is sensitive to her son's great potential and ensures that he will actualize it completely to fulfill his mission and role in life. We learn that it is the mother who crowns her son from an explicit verse in the Song of Songs, "With the crown that his mother crowned him on his wedding day"[3].

In the verse about the creation of the world, "*Havayah* with wisdom founded the earth, with understanding He founded the heavens,"[4] there are four elements: wisdom, understanding, heaven and earth. These four elements parallel the four letters in God's essential four-letter Name, *Havayah*. wisdom and understanding parallel the *yud* and *hei* in God's Name and are also known as the father and mother principles. Heaven and

---

3. Song of Songs 3:11.
4. Proverbs 3:19.

earth parallel the two letters *vav* and *hei* in *Havayah*. They are like the father and mother's son and daughter.[5] Together, the son and the daughter represent the fulfillment of the *mitzvah*, "to be fruitful and multiply."[6]

Thus, the nuclear family consists of the father, mother, son and daughter. The verse says that "*Havayah* with wisdom founded the earth"—it is wisdom that founds the earth is the earth's foundation, specifically the father who is connected to his daughter, who represents *malchut* (kingdom). The father concerns himself with his daughter in the same manner that the mother concerns herself with her son. Conversely, "with understanding He founded the heavens,"—the heavens, the *vav* of the Name *Havayah*, the Small Countenance, the attributes of the heart, are established and nurtured by the mother, who represents understanding.

On this foundation, the Arizal explained[7] that the crown of the Small Countenance—the crown of the son, of the attributes of the heart, is made of the *tiferet* (beauty) of the mother principle. The foundation of the mother becomes the heart of the son, but the crown of the son comes from the mother's *tiferet*. Rebbetzin Chanah had *tiferet*, and with it, she made sure to crown her son with the crown that fit him.

Every son has the crown that fits him, "All of Israel are the children of kings"[8] (in the *Zohar* the reading is: "All of Israel are kings"[9]), which is the context with which every person should lead (in his home and on his life-mission). The mother has the sensitivity to identify the crown and tends to its actualization.

---

5. *Yevamot* 61b.

6. Genesis 1:28.

7. *Eitz Chaim* 21:3.

8. *Baba Metzia* 113b.

9. *Tikunnei Zohar* introduction and *Zohar* II, 26b.

The Rebbe was aware that his crown came from his mother (ever since he became a bar-*mitzvah* at age 13, even before the *shidduch* with the daughter of the Rebbe Rayatz was concluded. Since then, his mother did not see his back, as above). The Rebbe was grateful to his mother and was careful to always keep his relationship with her face to face—turning his face to his mother and receiving inspiration from her for the fulfillment of his leadership role.

The mother prepares the crown of her son. She gives him a feeling that is above reason and consciousness (otherwise known as the superconscious crown), which tells him from which things he should back off and in which direction he should go. That is a good reason not to turn our backs on our mothers—to receive inspiration from them as to which direction to progress in life, including the direction that will ultimately lead us to our true, fitting crown.

When the Rebbe Couldn't Get a Sound out of the Shofar

Before *Rosh Hashanah* one year in the 1950s, a Jew who we will call Chaim asked a family in Crown Heights, New York, near the Lubavitcher Rebbe's headquarters if they could host him for the upcoming holy days. Chaim was anxious to participate in the Rebbe's shofar blowing during the *Rosh Hashanah* prayers. He had been married for nine years and he and his wife had not been blessed with children. Chaim knew that before the Lubavitcher Rebbe blew the shofar on *Rosh Hashanah,* he would pray for all the people who had turned to him for a blessing. He wanted to be there, as close to the Rebbe as possible, to be blessed with a child.

Chaim's hosts advised him to get to prayers early to find a place near the Rebbe. Chaim situated himself in a good spot and waited.

The Rebbe came down to the synagogue with a number of *shofar* as was his custom. With the most earnest and serious face, the Rebbe began reciting the chapters of Psalms customary before the blowing of the *shofar.* Chaim said every word with the Rebbe.

All seven repetitions of chapter 47 in Psalms. He was intensely focused. The congregation was absolutely silent. All eyes were on the Rebbe. All thoughts were hinged on the success of the shofar blowing.

The Rebbe said the blessing on the *shofar* and raised the first shofar to his lips. No sound came out. Absolute silence. He took another *shofar*. No sound. The anxiety in the congregation mounted. The third shofar. No sound. Confusion and dismay filled the hearts of all those present. Chaim, who was standing near the Rebbe, remained intensely focused. He and his wife had been anticipating a child for 9 years. All his hopes were pinned on the Rebbe, that in merit of his *shofar* blowing, they would have children.

The tension was thick and pervasive. The Rebbe attempted to blow *shofar* after *shofar*, with no sound coming out. With all his personal pain, Chaim suddenly thought, "Perhaps my strong focus on salvation for myself is what is stopping the sounds from coming out." He turned to God and said to Him, "Dear God, I forfeit my deep intention and prayers for a child for the good of the congregation."

At that very moment, the Rebbe took another *shofar* and perfect sounds came out. Chaim cried profusely. One year later, Chaim and his wife were blessed with a child. A few years later, he brought the little boy to get a cup of blessing from the Rebbe. Chaim had not told his story to anyone. He passed before the Rebbe. There was all of about a second to stand before the Rebbe before the next person's turn. The

> Rebbe looked at Chaim and asked, "Is this the child from the blowing of the *shofar*?"

We give birth to Mashiach during the blowing of the *shofar*. But he only comes when we remove our thoughts from him. Mashiach is essential for us, similar to the way Chaim felt about having children. But Chaim's focus was so strong that he created tremendous pressure. It was as if he was suffocating the Rebbe himself—so much so that he could not get a sound out of the *shofar*. Chaim had to let go.

We may be over-focused on all the good things that we want and need. Those goals may truly be worthy. But they are liable to suffocate the *shofar*. By letting go for a moment, all the effort we exerted earlier will suddenly bear fruit. The Ba'al Shem Tov says that the most important products and emanation from a *mitzvah* only occur after the *mitzvah* is complete. We may think that nothing happened after all our effort. But when we desist, the Divine light manifests. Our efforts have the power to draw down and reveal Divine light, but only once we let go.

There are two revealed and two concealed dimensions of prayer, corresponding to the letters of God's Name, *Havayah*, as reflected in the verse, "The concealed things are for *Havayah*, our God and the revealed are for us and our children [Deuteronomy 29:28]

Our prayers for anything we need in life are in the *sefirah* of kingdom, as the verse says, "I am prayer." Kingdom is likened to the moon, which lacks an autonomous source of light. It is always praying to be filled, like King David, who lived with the pervasive feeling that he was about to die, and continuously prayed for life anew. To pray for what we need a great *mitzvah* in the Torah. This is the final, or lower *hei* of *Havayah*, the lower level of the revealed dimension of God's Name.

The Ba'al Shem Tov taught that even when we have a personal problem, it should first be connected to the congregation or the world. So if we are in pain, we should pray to alleviate the pain of the congregation. This does entail leaving our personal space a bit, but does not require us to forgo what we need. When we ascend to the level of the congregation, we are ascending from the lower *hei* of *Havayah* to the *vav* of *Havayah*, the second letter of the revealed dimension of God's Name.

Sometimes, however, this is not enough. There are things that we have to release altogether. When we ascend to the level of release in favor of the congregation, we have entered the concealed dimension. Chaim was sure that he should have a child. In the revealed dimension, this is indeed the reason for his life. Yet, God knows better. To forgo our own personal redemption for the interest of the many, inducts us into the concealed dimension, the first, or upper *hei* in God's Name, *Havayah*. The concealed dimension itself has two levels and the first *hei* is considered its lower level.What if, however, there is a situation that requires the complete re-alignment of nature in order to be resolved? What does the *tzaddik* have to forgo in order bless someone with something that contradicts the laws of nature?

According to the Ba'al Shem Tov, the *tzaddik* would have to forgo his reward in the World to Come. This is an earthshaking thought. This is a novel situation in which an individual is willing to sacrifice himself for another individual. Forgoing one's own good for the good of the congregation corresponds to the *hei,* which is also a symbol for the World to Come. Thus, to intercede so that a couple who is clinically infertile can have children despite the laws of nature,requires the *tzaddik* to go beyond the first *hei,* to forfeit his World to Come. It requires, as it were, a recreation of reality. The ability to do so comes from masculine Abba the *sefirah* of wisdom, associated with the *yud* of God's Name *Havayah*. This is the higher level of the concealed dimension of God's Name.

To summarize, the first, lower *hei* level of prayer is when a person prays for himself. Above that is the *vav* level of connecting one's needs with those of the congregation. Above that is the upper *hei* level of forgoing one's needs for the congregation (this requires removal of our thoughts from the need). Finally, the highest, *yud* level is to forgo one's needs for another individual.

What might be a fifth level to this model? To sacrifice my own benefit for the sake of God's. This is even higher than forfeiting my own benefit for some other person. God is the greatest "individual." Forgoing my own benefit completely for the benefit of another Jew is the inner aspect of giving oneself over entirely to God.

The *Or Hachaim* and the Lion

Rabbi Chaim Ben-Atar, known as the holy *Or Hachaim* for his famous commentary on the Torah, was born in 5456 (1696) in Morocco. Even as a young man, he was known as a holy and scholarly man of God. Near the end of 5501 (1741), he made *aliyah* to the Land of Israel, settling first in Acre and afterward in Tiberias and Peki'in. By 5502 he had moved to Jerusalem, establishing his yeshivah, Midreshet Knesset Yisrael. The Ba'al Shem Tov said that the holy *Or Hachaim* was the Mashiach of the generation. The *Or Hachaim* himself alluded to this, writing, "the name of the Mashiach is Chaim." His Torah commentary was honored throughout the Jewish world and particularly among the disciples of the Ba'al Shem Tov. The Rebbe Rayatz related that the *Or Hachaim* wrote his commentary from the Torah lessons that he would teach his daughters. The *Or Hachaim* passed away on the 15th of Tamuz, 5503 (1743) and is buried on the Mount of Olives in Jerusalem.

Rabbi Chaim Ben Atar made his way to the Land of Israel in a caravan of camels in the desert. Shabbat was approaching and the *Or Hachaim* asked the leaders of the caravan, who were Arabs, to stop and rest where they were so that he would not have to desecrate the Shabbat. They refused. The *Or Hachaim* decided that he would not continue with the caravan so as not to desecrate the Shabbat— despite the danger of wild animals, robbers and murderers in the desert. He desired to fulfill the words of the verse, "Abide every man in his place, no man may go out of his place on the seventh day" (Exodus 16:29) with self-sacrifice. When the Shabbat arrived, a large lion approached the *Or Hachaim*, and laid down next to him for the entire Shabbat. Obviously, no robbers or murderers wanted to come near the *Or Hachaim* and his ominous friend. When the Shabbat was over, the lion rose up on his feet, bent his head down as if he was bowing, signaling the *Or Hachaim* to climb up onto his back. Rabbi Chaim sat himself on the lion's back and the lion raced toward the caravan, depositing his passenger safely back with the group.

* * *

At first, it seems that the *Or Hachaim* practically committed suicide. The desert is a distinctly dangerous place and it does not seem reasonable to stay there alone. Recklessness and suicide are a blemish in the *sefirah* of kingdom, about which it is said that "its feet descend unto death" (Proverbs 5:5). But in truth, this story is a rectification of kingdom, because all was done with self-sacrifice for the sake of honoring the Shabbat queen. By fulfilling the directive, "Abide every man in his place" the holy *Or Hachaim* precluded the danger of kingdom's legs, which as noted, "descend unto death." On the contrary, he was able to nullify the evil inclination for suicide (and perhaps was able to do so for all Israel).

In general, this entire story is kingly: The lion, king of the jungle, sits and guards the *Or Hachaim* throughout the Shabbat, which is a very regal thing to do, also cause for a rectification of the *sefirah* of kingdom. After Shabbat, the lion bows down to him and takes him on his back—similar to King Solomon, who, according to the sages, would fly from place to place on the wings of his eagle. In this story, we see the messianic, kingly character of the holy *Or Hachaim*.

Rebbe Shlomo of Karlin: The Invisible Rebbe

The holy Rebbe Shlomo Halevi of Karlin, was born to Rabbi Nachum in 5494 (1738). He was a preeminent student of the Maggid of Mezritch and of Rebbe Aharon Hagadol of Karlin. After the passing of Rebbe Aharon, Rebbe Shlomo assumed his mantle in Karlin. He was known for his powerful devotion to God and became famous as a miracle worker motivated by genuine self-sacrifice. His prayers were fiery, he gave all his money to charity and his Torah learning was enthusiastic and stormy. The great sages of his generation admired him and he had a particularly close relationship with the Alter Rebbe of Chabad. His primary students include Rebbe Asher of Stolin, Rebbe Uri (the Saraf) of Strelisk and Rebbe Mordechai of Lechovitch.

In the year 5552 (1791) a Russian soldier shot Rebbe Shlomo while he stood devoutly in prayer. Rebbe Shlomo suffered for five days, until his soul ascended to heaven on the 22nd of Tamuz. Many considered him to be the Mashiach the son of Joseph. His teachings were compiled in the book *Shema Shlomo.*

Before settling in Karlin, Rebbe Shlomo traveled from place to place in White Russia, searching for a suitable location for his chassidic court. On one of his trips, he came to a small village called Postov and stayed with a wealthy man called Reb Yehudah of Postov. Reb Yehuda was not a *chassid*, but he agreed to host Rebbe Shlomo. In the morning, Rebbe Shlomo asked his host where he could find a *mikveh* (ritual bath). Slightly cynical, Reb Yehuda replied that there was no men's *mikveh* in the town, as there is no obligation to have one, according to Jewish law. "Is there a river nearby where I can immerse?" Rebbe Shlomo asked, but this too, Reb Yehuda answered in the negative. "Is there at least a well here in which I can immerse?" the Rebbe asked. "There is one well in the entire town, but it is in the yard of the priest, who hates Jews like Haman. Only he has a well," Reb Yehuda summed it up.

Much to Reb Yehuda's surprise, Rebbe Shlomo ordered his assistants to gather some sheets and to prepare for their short trip to the priest's yard. What the Rebbe says, the *chassidim* do and in no time, a whole company of *chassidim* and townspeople, with the Rebbe at their head, was marching down the road toward the priest's well. The Rebbe and his followers reached the priest's yard, opened the gate without asking, the *chassidim* spread the sheets around the well to partition it off and the Rebbe descended into the well to immerse, with the entire entourage waiting and watching this decidedly extraordinary sight.

The priest and his family were sitting on their porch when suddenly they saw a long line of townspeople and *chassidim* approaching their home and gathering around the well. The priest immediately called one of the spectators, who said to him, "Don't you see? Right in front of your eyes is a Jew who entered your yard, spread out sheets, and descended to immerse himself in your well!" The priest and his family did not see. But when he heard what had transpired, he was livid. He ran down to his yard with one intention only: to kill the Jew who had dared to immerse in his well. The priest furiously approached Rebbe Shlomo, and just a moment before he smote him, an inexplicable and terrifying fear descended upon him and he turned around and ran.

The priest did not give up so easily, though. He sent some of his bullies to the Rebbe's accommodations, but the same thing happened. The bullies entered in order to smite the Rebbe when they were also suddenly overcome by inexplicable terror, turned on their heels, and ran away.

The priest understood that the Rebbe was not just an ordinary person and that it was impossible to approach him, in addition to the fact that he had not been visible to him (as is told about Pinchas, who was like an angel, who the messengers of the king of Jericho could not see. Israel is, in essence, invisible. They see but are not seen)!

Eventually, the priest made his way sheepishly to Reb Yehuda Postover's home and begged him to request of the *tzaddik*, from the holy man, that he should just allow him to see his face. Reb Yehuda Postover submitted the request, but the Rebbe adamantly refused. An impure, uncircumcised evil person should see his face? Under no circumstances.

All that had transpired awakened a great question for Reb Yehuda. He approached Rebbe Shlomo and said that he had a question for him and that he would thank the Rebbe if he would be kind enough to answer. "How could it be that this priest, an evil person, a Jew-hater like Haman, uncircumcised and impure, recognized that you are a righteous, holy person, while I, a Jew, still do not recognize this—even after all that has transpired?

Rebbe Shlomo answered him simply: "You do not belong to me, but rather to the Maggid of Liozna (the Alter Rebbe). Go to him." Reb Yehuda did indeed travel to the Alter Rebbe and ultimately became one of his greatest *chassidim*.

* * *

Rectification for Every Soul

This entire story is about the holiness of the covenant, personal holiness. A person who has achieved a state of personal holiness has no reason to fear wild animals and if needed, has the miraculous ability to see and not be seen. In addition, this is a story about the custom of *chassidim* to immerse in a *mikveh*— in order to purify their state of personal holiness to ever-greater heights—and there is no limit to purity. Why does the *tzaddik*, who is rectified and holy, with no hint of impurity, have to immerse in a *mikveh*? Because there are limitless levels of purity, and every immersion is like an ascent from one Garden of Eden to a higher Garden of Eden.

This story also teaches us about the ability to recognize the "*tzaddik*, the foundation of the world." Different people will identify different pious people as a *tzaddik*. With a bit of thought on the content of this story, a deep and important understanding crystallizes: That Jew-hating, Hamanic priest "belonged" to Rebbe Shlomo of Karlin while the Jew, Reb Yehuda, did not belong to him, but rather, to the Alter Rebbe. What does this mean? It turns out that everyone, including non—Jews and even the most depraved evil people in the world—is connected to a *tzaddik*.

This is part of the rectification process. The *tzaddik* has the Divine power to rectify those souls to a certain extent. Rebbe Shlomo performed a miracle in the priest's yard. He did not allow him to see him, yet nonetheless, a certain rectification for the priest, who recognized the Rebbe's holiness, did take place (as Reb Yehuda Postover saw that the priest recognized the Rebbe's holiness deep in his soul).

When an evil non-Jew recognizes the holiness of a Jew, it is a sign that he belongs to him. This is one of the foundations of Chassidut: Just as "There is no place void of God," so, the same is true for Knesset Yisrael, the holy *Shechinah*, God's Indwelling Presence: There is no reality in the world, even in the most impure place, that does not have a relevance to a Jewish soul. Even the most impure thing in the world is relevant to the rectification of some Jew, somewhere. If it is a holy Jew, the non-Jew also has some sort of affinity to him and the ability to recognize his holiness. Although Rebbe Shlomo chased the priest away, he did have some connection to him.

Rebbe Shlomo did not settle in Postov. So why did God bring him there as part of his 42 journeys? We can say that it was in order to send Reb Yehuda to the Alter Rebbe. But it was also to rectify the evil priest so that he would recognize that there is a holy Jew. (Sometimes, the rectification is the extraction of the spark. In this story, the rectification was his recognition of Rebbe Shlomo's holiness). This is a type of Kiddush Hashem, sanctification of God's Name. Turning Reb Yehuda Postover into a *chassid* of Rebbe Shlomo of Karlin is not a sanctification of God's Name. But the priest's recognition of Rebbe Shlomo's holiness certainly is.

Rebbe Shlomo of Karlin:
Misers and Charity

Rebbe Shlomo of Karlin was once on a journey. The time came to stop for the night. Two inns were available in that town.

"Who are the owners of the inns?" Rebbe Shlomo asked. "What are they like?"

One of them is a strictly observant Jew," his aide answered. "He studies Torah and prays regularly. But he is a terrible miser and the poor do not dare to step on his threshold, for they know that he will not let them in. The second innkeeper is actually quite generous and gives freely to all those who request charity. He is, however, an unfaithful husband, may God have mercy."

"Let us turn to the inn of the generous innkeeper," Rebbe Shlomo decided. "Although both innkeepers suffer from serious faults, the generous innkeeper is closer to repentance than the miser."

* * *

Rebbe Shlomo understood that the generous yet adulterous

innkeeper, due to his more easy-going nature, was closer to returning to God than the strictly observant miser. As a rule, Rebbe Shlomo was not very fond of people who were very strict and rigid in their observance of Judaism. The Alter Rebbe of Chabad even reproved him for this, saying that one has to seek out the good points in the rigid, strictly observant just as one would seek out the good points in the simple Jews of whom the Ba'al Shem Tov was so fond.

In Rebbe Shlomo's worldview, the generous innkeeper had a serious problem with his evil inclination. But he was happy to do favors and good deeds for others and so was more likely to repent. On the other hand, he saw the miser as being from the *sitra achra*, (the other side). Even though he was an observant Jew, he was under the control of the Satan and had an evil eye.

What is a miser and what is so terrible about him? He is only concerned with himself. He wants to keep everything for himself and is not willing to yield to anybody else. The filling of the letter *vav* (ו) is spelled *vav, alef, vav* (ואו) and is an acronym for "yield, love, and be compassionate" (וַתֵּר אֱהֹב וְרַחֵם). *Vav* is one of the letters in God's Essential Name, *Havayah,* and according to some opinions, it is the main letter in God's Name. The letter *vav* is a letter of connection and also a letter that transforms the tense of a verb from past to future and vice versa, thus exemplifying the power to transform darkness into light and bitterness into sweetness.[1] And that is what connecting, giving, loving and being compassionate are all about.

What can we learn from the teaching that being a miser is worse than being an adulterer and that a miser actually belongs to the *sitra achra*? In our story, we see that a consummately evil person is not willing to give charity. He is not willing to give anything of himself. A consummately evil person is a

---

1.   *Zohar* I, 4a.

consummate miser, meaning that he is not charitable with his wealth. Let us construct a model to explain the miserly nature of a consummate *rasha* (evil person) by considering the *mitzvah* of charity. Specifically, we will gauge the different types of people based on the measure of their charity. These include a consummate *rasha*, a non-consummate *rasha*, an intermediate person, a non-consummate *tzaddik*, a consummate *tzaddik* and a *ba'al teshuvah* (a penitent).

It is written[2] that the average measure of charity is fulfilled by following the letter of the law regarding charity and giving one-tenth of one's earnings to charity. The highest level of charity is when one gives a fifth of one's earnings, as the sages in Usha (where they gathered after the destruction of the second Temple and the exile of the Sanhedrin) determined, "He who wishes to give with abandon shall not give more than one fifth."[3] Thus, a person who gives nothing is consummately evil and a person who gives less than a tenth is non-consummately evil. A person who is diligent about giving exactly a tenth from all his earnings is considered an intermediate person (a *beinoni*). A person who gives more than one-tenth but less than one fifth is a non-consummate *tzaddik* and a person who gives a fifth is a consummate *tzaddik*.

Chassidut encourages us to give even more than a fifth by choosing to see ourselves as a penitent. The penitent is not limited to a fifth because he is giving in order to return to God and save his soul.[4] The *Tanya* also teaches[5] that even if a person is abjectly poor, he must also give generously, according to his ability. The *Tanya* adds that if you know of a poor person who

---

2.   Maimonides *Hilchot matnot aniyim* 7:5.

3.   *Ketubot* 50a.

4.   See *Tanya, Igeret Hateshuva* chapter 3.

5.   *Tanya Igeret Hakodesh* 16.

is not able to put food on his table, while you need money for luxuries, you must forgo the luxuries and give beyond a fifth, explaining that this, the fifth measure of charity, becomes the letter of the law in a case that a person is so poor that he literally has nothing.

REBBE SHLOMO OF KARLIN: TRULY NO SPACE VOID OF GOD

Once, the daughter of a Torah scholar married, but after a short time, her husband disappeared, leaving her an *agunah*. An *agunah* is a woman who is "anchored" to her husband. Due to the fact that his whereabouts are unknown, he is unavailable (or refuses) to give her a divorce, so she remains bound to him until it can either be proven that he is no longer alive, or until he is located and gives his wife a proper divorce. Nobody knew where the young husband was, or if he was alive or dead. The family searched for him extensively and did all that they could, but nothing helped. After all their efforts, the Torah scholar's wife turned to him and said, "Nothing else seems to have helped. You have to go to the *tzaddik*, Rebbe Shlomo of Karlin. Perhaps the salvation will come from him." The husband, who was not a *chassid* at all, reluctantly agreed to do her bidding. His concern for his daughter overpowered his concerns about the *chassidim*.

The father reached Rebbe Shlomo's home right when he was exiting the bathroom, before he had even managed to ritually wash his hands. A bit taken aback by the awkward situation and not sure quite what to do, the father went straight over to Rebbe Shlomo and blurted out, "My daughter is an *agunah*." Rebbe Shlomo pointed to a wagon standing nearby and said, "Her husband is sitting there in the wagon. Run over there quickly and you will find him."

A moment before running off in the direction of the wagon, the father turned once again to Rebbe Shlomo and asked in surprise, "You employ *ruach hakodesh* (Divine inspiration) before you even ritually wash your hands? How can that be?"

"You should know," Rebbe Shlomo answered him, "that the fact that *tzaddikim* see things from afar is not due to their *ruach hakodesh* at all. It is perfectly natural. Everybody in the world has clay on their eyes, which hides all that transpires. But for those who merit— God removes the clay. Once a person has ritually washed his hands and he is pure, he is required to study Torah and pray. He does not have time to look around at what is happening in the world. But when a *tzaddik* is in the bathroom, where he cannot pray and study, he has time to look at what is happening in the world. And so it was, when I was in the bathroom, I naturally—without *ruach hakodesh*—saw your errant son-in-law on the wagon."

* * *

Rebbe Shlomo began by teaching the father that he did not employ *ruach hakodesh*, but rather, this was a natural phenomenon, natural consciousness that is part of the innate, behavioral part of the soul. This is not something in which the *tzaddik* invests any special thought or effort. It is specifically in the bathroom, a place that is not relevant to Torah study or prayer, that the *tzaddik* can look at what is happening in the world. *Tzaddikim* do not need to read the newspaper in the bathroom, as some people do, because they see everything without the newspaper—much more in line with the truth than the dubious reports in the media. From their vantage point, they can orchestrate reality and do what needs to be done (as is written in other stories of *tzaddikim*, particularly about Rebbe Shlomo of Karlin).

One of the essential points of contention between *chassidim* and *mitnagdim* (those opposed to the teachings of Chassidut) in the early days of Chassidut was about the *tzimtzum*. The *mitnagdim* maintained that the contraction of energy performed by God (*tzimtzum*) in order to create a void space (called *hachallal hapanui*) in which to create the world is truly void of God, Heaven forbid. The *chassidim* countered that although we cannot see God, He is everywhere, just as He was before the *tzimtzum*, as explained at length in chassidic teachings. One of the 'accusations' of the *mitnagdim*—which seems strange to us today—was that the *chassidim*, who do not take the *tzimtzum* literally, but rather maintain that God is everywhere, also believe that God is in impure places like the bathroom. This, concluded the *mitnagdim*, contradicts the Torah, which teaches us not to study or pray in unclean places. This is also the source of the question that the father asked Rebbe Shlomo: How could he have *ruach hakodesh* after exiting the bathroom, before ritually washing his hands?

Chassidut explains that God is everywhere: "There is no place void of Him." Learning Torah and praying, however, are allowed only outside the bathroom. From this story we see that the bathroom is a kind of control room for *tzaddikim*, from where they can keep an eye on what is happening throughout the world.

On a deeper level, the unchaining of *agunot* (anchored women) is one of the Torah issues in which the *tzaddikim* and sages have invested the most time and effort, as is reflected in the many volumes of responsa on this topic throughout the generations (including in our generation, unchaining widows of fallen soldiers whose whereabouts are unknown). When a true sage is required to find a way to unbind a woman and save her from bondage (which is a type of saving her life) generally, he will prove that the husband is not alive. Unbinding the *agunah* is actually an entry into the *challal hapanui*, the space "void of God" as it were, outside the borders of holiness and certainty—in order to find the deceased husband (called a *challal* in Hebrew). The power to exit the boundaries of holiness belongs to the behavioral part of the soul, which corresponds to the three habitual *sefirot* of *netzach, hod* and *yesod*—victory, acknowledgment, and foundation.

The greatest Torah-based victory of a Torah adjudicator is to unchain an *agunah*. This also allows the soul of her deceased husband to ascend from the *challal hapanui* to the Garden of Eden (for the very fact that he is still anchoring his wife also damages his own soul).

While the Torah engages the *challal hapanui* and determines what is supposed to take place there (such as the determination in Jewish law that one should not learn Torah in the bathroom), the *tzaddik* who locates the living husband, such as Rebbe Shlomo in our story, penetrates the *challal hapanui* with the behavioral innate traits of his soul. He does so by means of a type of Divine inspiration, which, for him, is nothing more than natural consciousness, with the knowledge that the state of concealment is nothing more than superficial "clay on the eyes," and that in truth, God is in every place. The *tzaddik* can see Him naturally, and reveal to the world that there is no place void of Him.

Rebbe Shlomo of Karlin: Double Gain

Once Rebbe Shlomo of Karlin was traveling in a wagon with his disciples. They reached the summit of a very steep mountain. The wagon-driver lost control of the horses and the wagon began to career down the mountain at breakneck speed. The passengers were shouting and crying. Rebbe Shlomo was immersed in his service of cleaving to God and was originally unaware of what was transpiring. Suddenly, the extreme situation penetrated his consciousness and he momentarily stopped his Divine service as he became aware of the life-threatening danger. Immediately he heard a voice from heaven that declared that he had just lost his entire portion in the world to come. This had been a trial from heaven, similar to trials that the Ba'al Shem Tov had experienced on his journey to the Land of Israel. Rebbe Shlomo was expected to fear nothing but God.

When he heard the voice from heaven, Rebbe Shlomo quickly announced that he does not accept the decree. The *tzaddik* claimed that this verdict came from the heavenly house of study. But he was not willing to accept their verdict. Instead he insisted on a verdict from God Himself. When he said this, something happened in heaven. Rebbe Shlomo heard a different voice announcing that if so, we will return the *tzaddik's* world to come.

When Rebbe Shlomo related this to his disciples, he said that at that moment he gained two things: He merited to greet the *Shechinah* (God's Presence) and he also merited the world to come.

* * *

This story reflects the fear of falling into the abyss that was caused by the spiritual fall of the *tzaddik,* who momentarily stopped his service of cleaving to God. In the end, it turned out to be a "descent for the sake of an ascent." He was told that due to his descent he had lost his connection to the supernal mother figure, *(imma ila'ah),* also referred to as the World to Come, but he insisted on hearing his verdict directly from God.

This story points us to the story of the breaking of the Tablets on the 17th of Tamuz. On this same day a few years later, Rebbe Shlomo was shot and eventually died of his wounds, sanctifying God's Name. In his daily calendar with aphorisms, *"Hayom Yom,"* the Lubavitcher Rebbe writes the difference between the first and second Tablets. The second Tablets were superior to the first—so much so that after Moses broke the first Tablets, God said to him, "More power to you for breaking them." In our story, Rebbe Shlomo loses his first level but then merits-regaining his World to Come—a double advantage over his original state.

Rebbe Moshe Teitelbaum of Satmer

Rabbi Moshe Teitelbaum, the father of the Siget-Satmer dynasty and one of the main disseminators of Chassidut in Hungary, was called the *Yismach Moshe*, the name of one of the books that he authored. Rabbi Teitelbuam was born in 5519/1759 in Galicia to Rabbi Tzvi Hirsch and Chanah. He studied Torah with his uncle, Rabbi Yosef of Kolvesov and Rabbi Aryeh Yehudah Halevi, the Rabbi of Strizov. At the age of 25, Rabbi Teitelbaum was appointed as the Rabbi of Shinwa in Galicia and later, as the Rabbi of Oheli in Hungary. Upon the influence of his father-in-law, author of the *'Aryeh Debai Ilaai,'* Rabbi Teitelbaum became a *chassid* of the Chozeh (Seer) of Lublin. He would also travel to study with the Maggid of Mezritch, Rabbi Mendeleh of Rimanov and the Ohev Yisrael of Apta. Rabbi Teitelbaum wrote many books, including *Yismach Moshe* on the Bible, Responsa *Heshiv Moshe, Yayin Harokeach* on Pirkei Avot and more. His disciples included: His son, Rabbi Elazar Nissan, Rabbi Yoel Ashkenazi, author of *"Melo Haro'im",* Rabbi Menachem Mendel Peannet of Desh and Rabbi Tzvi Hirsch of Liska. Rabbi Teitelbaum passed away on 28 Tamuz, 5601 (1841) and he is buried next to his wife in Oheli.

Happiness and Sadness Simultaneously in the Heart

The following story was told by Rabbi Teitelbaum's grandson, the *"Yitav Lev:"*

When the *Yismach Moshe* was learning the ways of Chassidut, the chassidic custom to always be happy perplexed him. After all, it is explicitly written in the

Code of Jewish Law, "It is befitting for every person who fears Heaven to be sorrowful and worried in his heart over the destruction of the Holy Temple!" Before one of his trips to his mentor, the *Chozeh* of Lublin, the Yismach Moshe prayed to God: "You know my thoughts and the depths of my heart... Help me so that when I come to the holy *tzaddik*, he will answer my question."

Immediately when he entered the *Chozeh's* room, the *Chozeh* said to him, "Why are you looking so weak today? True, it is written in the Code of Jewish Law that 'It is befitting for every person who fears Heaven...' But the wise man (in the Duties of the Heart by Rabbi Behayai Ibn Pekuda 1050-1120) has already said, 'Jubilation on my face and mourning in my heart'..."

Let us pause this story in the middle of the words of the *Chozeh* of Lublin in order to consider them carefully. We can be amazed by the spiritual sight of the *Chozeh*, who resolved his disciple's question before he even opened his mouth. But how can we reconcile the two opposites? How can we be 'sorrowful and worried' in the words of the Code of Jewish Law while simultaneously being happy and even jubilant?

The *Chozeh* of Lublin quoted the "wise man" in the book, "The Duties of the Heart," the most important *(ethics)* book of ethics written during the era of the *Rishonim*. "Jubilation on my face and mourning in my heart." I conduct myself with joy, say *'Lechaim,"* sing and dance, but in my inner chambers, deep in my heart, I am in a state of great sorrow.

The division between an external façade of joy and internal seriousness and concern, is actually taken from the inner world of God, Himself, as in the words of Jeremiah, "And if you do not hear it, my soul shall weep in secret (*mistarim*) because of pride, and my eyes shall weep and shed a tear, for the flock of God has been captured. In the Talmud (*Chagigah* 5:2), the Sages explain this verse as follows:

"The Holy Blessed One has a place called *mistarim* ('secret,' as in the verse above) [and it is there that He cries]. What is 'because of pride?' Rabbi Shmuel Bar Yitzchak said, because of the pride of Israel that was taken from them and given to the non-Jews. Rabbi Shmuel Bar Nachman said, because of the pride of the kingdom of Heaven. And is there crying before the Holy, Blessed One? Rabbi Papa said, there is no sadness before the Holy Blessed One, as it says, "Majestic aura and splendor before Him, vigor and exquisite joy in His place!" This is not a difficulty, one place refers to His inner chambers and the other place refers to His outer chambers."

In God's inner chambers, in the secret place called '*mistarim*,' He figuratively enters His inner self and cries over the destruction of the Temple and the lowly state of His beloved children. But outwardly, in the place where He is revealed to His creations, he shows a smiling face of "vigor and exquisite joy."

This fits the description of the *chassid,* who has "jubilation on his face and mourning in his heart." On the outside, he fulfills the directive, "Serve God with joy," (Psalms 100:2) and as a true 'happy *chassid*' he does not sink into lethargy or laziness for even a moment. Inside, however, his heart is broken. In the inner sanctum of his soul, he cries bitterly over all his shortcomings and over the sorrow of the *Shechinah*. In the place that he feels the depth of the exile, he is engulfed with mourning. (The Hebrew word for 'exile' is '*galut*,' which has the same numerical value as '*avelut*,' which means 'mourning.')

A *chassid* like this is a fitting 'vessel' for the revelation of the secrets of the Torah: "We only convey the secrets of the Torah to someone whose heart worries inside him." His "heart worries inside him" and his "jubilation is on his face."

Nevertheless, we may still think that there is some sort of 'division of authority:' Joy is only external while in truth, in the deepest depths of the soul, the heart is irreparably broken, without a drop of joy. Is this the true face of the situation? Is all the joy nothing more than an act? Is the service of God with joy not true and heartfelt?

Let us continue the story:

> The Seer of Lublin continued: "Believe me, I say the Midnight Lamentations with tears and mourning. But nonetheless, it is all with joy. And this is what our holy Rabbi, Rebbe Shmelkeh of Nicholsberg, taught us. There is a parable of a king who was taken captive and exiled to a distant land. The king rested from his long journey at the home of one of his loving subjects. When the subject saw the king in captivity, he cried uncontrollably. Nevertheless, he was happy that the king was staying with him. And the moral of the story is clear, for the *Shechinah* is with us..."
>
> These words of the Seer completely reassured his disciple, who, from then on, cleaved to his holy rabbi. (Perhaps this is the reason why he was called "Yismach Moshe," which means, "Moshe will be happy," after he merited to understand the secret of joy.)

The *Chozeh* of Lublin testified about himself—"Believe me,"— and we certainly do believe him—that he said the Midnight Lamentations with tears and mourning. When saying the

Midnight Lamentations one is directed to "sit on the ground… remove his shoes and put ashes on his head, in the place designated for the tefillin. Then one recites chapters of Psalms that are lamentations: "On the shores of Babylon, there we sat and also cried…God, non-Jews have entered Your Land…" remember what has happened to us…"

What happens then, when the Rebbe is sitting on the ground and crying over the destruction, over the exile of the *Shechinah*? On the surface, all the outward joy has completely disappeared and all that is left is the sorrow, alone, "In *mistarim* my soul cries." The joyful mask was removed and he cries profusely. But that is not the case! The *Chozeh* added in the same breath, "Nevertheless, it is all with joy. Even in the midst of the Midnight Lamentations, I am happy!"

In order to explain this, the *Chozeh* uses the wondrous parable of his rabbi, Rebbe Shmelkeh (who was one of the greatest disciples of the Maggid of Mezritch), about the king going into exile. Here it is already clear that the two apparently conflicting emotions, happiness and worry, are in the heart simultaneously. The loving subject of the king "cries uncontrollably" because he sees the king in his present situation, but on the other hand, at the very same moment, he is filled with silent joy that he has the merit to host the king in his own private home.

This secret is written in the holy Zohar: "On one side of the heart there is sorrow and worry and on the other side, vigor and exquisite joy, happiness and jubilation. Both exist in the heart simultaneously.

The Wondrous Mission of the Arizal's Students

The holy Rabbi Yitzchak Luria (the Arizal) was born in Jerusalem in 5294 (1533). When he was a young boy, his father passed away and he moved with his mother to the home of his uncle in Egypt. In Egypt, he learned Torah from Rabbi Betzalel Ashkenazi, author of the *Shitah Mekubetzet* and from the Radbaz. While in Egypt, he delved deeply into the holy Zohar. Elijah the Prophet was revealed to him and he discovered a new, deep method in Kabbalah. As per the instructions of Elijah the Prophet, the Arizal made *aliyah* to Tzfat and taught his method of Kabbalah to Rabbi Chaim Vital, who wrote his teachings in book form. The Arizal's most famous book, which includes the main points of his method, is *"Eitz Chaim"*. The Arizal passed away at the early age of 38 and is buried in Tzfat. The Arizal's method and teachings of Kabbalah have been accepted by all branches of the Nation of Israel until this very day.

The Arizal was the first to reveal awesome secrets of Kabbalah, never before revealed in the world. Not only was there opposition to him in Heaven, but down on earth, as well, there were some *tzaddikim* and rabbis who thought that it was forbidden to reveal these secrets to the public—and that even if God had revealed those secrets to him, he should just keep them to himself. There were even great rabbis who considered excommunicating him. The greatest rabbi who wanted to excommunicate him was the

Maharshal, Rabbi Shlomo Luria, who was also a relative of the Arizal. The Maharshal was the Chief Rabbi of Lublin, the foremost center of European Jewry at that time. He was considered the Torah giant of his generation and he was very unhappy that the Arizal was revealing secrets of Kabbalah. He joined with the Ram"a—the famous commentary on the *Shulchan Aruch*, according to which we determine Jewish law and who lived in his community in Lublin, and added another important rabbi in order to have three rabbis necessary to excommunicate the holy Ari.

The Arizal saw all of this with his *ruach hakodesh* (Divine inspiration). In order to prevent the excommunication from ever happening, he sent two of his students—one, his distinguished student, Rabbi Chaim Vital, and an additional student—on a mission. The Arizal did not take this action to preserve his personal honor. He was revealing the secrets of Kabbalah for a reason—to hasten the redemption—and this had to be safeguarded.

How were the Arizal's students supposed to quickly get from Tzfat to Lublin? For that, the holy Ari arranged a cloud.

The students boarded the cloud at the Ari's behest and quickly arrived in Lublin (performing another important mission on the way), just in time for the Friday afternoon prayers. Although they looked pious, nobody knew who they were. When the Silent Prayer was over, the *shaliach tzibbur* leading the prayer waited for the Maharshal to complete his prayer, as was the custom. The entire congregation was respectfully waiting when one of the Arizal's students said to the synagogue's beadle, "Why do we have to wait for this rabbi, when all that he is doing now is thinking about the wheel of a wagon?" Prayer is the time to think about God, but this pious-looking man is saying that hundreds of Jews are waiting for the rabbi, who is thinking about a wagon wheel.

The beadle was terribly upset. They may look pious, but they are shaming the rabbi. As he did not know what to do, the beadle went to the rabbi, himself, told him what had occurred and asked him what to do. After all, insulting the rabbi is an insult to the Torah that he learns, and the rabbi must punish them.

The Maharshal carefully listened to the beadle and said not to do anything to the guests. Later, he explained that on every Friday afternoon, before he concludes the Silent Prayer and takes his three steps backwards, he reviews in his head all the rulings on Jewish law that he had handed over during that week to ensure that he had not erred, Heaven forbid. He related that he did this review at the end of the Silent Prayer, for then his head was the clearest. "At the end of the Silent Prayer," he said, "I was thinking about one of the cases that I had this week, which revolved around a wagon wheel. So these two guests have *ruach hakodesh*. They knew what I was thinking."

The Maharshal invited the two important guests to spend Shabbat with him in his home. When cutting the *challah* loaf after Kiddush, something strange happened. An ant had apparently crawled into the *challah,* and the Maharshal had cut it in half. It was an awkward moment. One of the guests, who was sitting next to the Maharshal took his scarf and passed it before the rabbi's eyes. Suddenly, he saw the ant as if it was the size of a camel. The Maharshal was very taken aback. An ant in the *challah* was bad enough, but when it looked the size of a camel, it was truly frightening. The guest then took two *challah* loaves out of his large pockets. These were special loaves, still warm as if they had just been removed from the oven, similar to the shewbread in the Holy Temple. The pious guest told the Maharshal that these were gifts from his holy rabbi, the Ari. He continued to tell the Maharshal that they had come from Tzfat on a cloud. The Arizal had seen with his *ruach hakodesh* that there would be a problem with your *challah,* so he sent you two special, heavenly *challah* loaves, which have the holiness of the Temple shewbread.

The Maharshal began to wonder if it was really correct to excommunicate the holy Ari. He asked the two guests to accompany him to his cellar. The Maharshal himself was also a great Kabbalist—but he kept that fact hidden. He did not learn or teach Kabbalah in public. In the cellar, he began to expound upon a deep Kabbalistic thought.

The Ari's students listened to the Maharshal's explanation and then Rabbi Chaim Vital opened his mouth and just said the first verse of the Torah: "In the beginning God created the heavens and the earth." At that moment, the Maharshal suddenly felt and saw that the heavens were created anew and the earth was created anew (as will be the case when the Mashiach comes—there will be new heavens and a new earth). The Maharshal understood that the power of the Torah of the student of the Ari was much greater than his own power. When he spoke, nothing was created, but when the student said just one verse, a new heaven and earth were created.

This convinced the Maharshal not to excommunicate the holy Ari. Excommunication can only be performed by someone greater than the subject of the excommunication, and the Maharshal understood that the Ari was greater than he, and if so, he apparently had the power and permission from Heaven to reveal the secrets of Kabbalah to the Nation of Israel.

* * *

This is a wondrous story, from which we learn that sometimes a *tzaddik* must invest tremendous effort in order not to be misunderstood: "And you shall be clean from God and from Israel." The greatest rabbi of the generation, the Arizal's cousin, was planning to excommunicate him. In order to prevent that, and in order for the Maharshal to understand just who the Ari was, he performed an entirely supernatural act, thus revealing his stature.

Sometimes, not only does the *tzaddik* have to reveal his stature, but he must even glorify himself. In this case, this was in order to prevent his excommunication, which could have been very damaging for the Nation of Israel and postponed the redemption. For this reason, the Ari went to great lengths to publicize himself with supernatural means. He sent his students on a cloud and gave them shewbread. The Arizal also allowed his student, Rabbi Chaim Vital, to say words of Torah from which the Maharshal would see how a new heaven and earth were created. This is a very unconventional way of operating, relevant only to a *tzaddik* who has broad *da'at*, knows himself, and can use self-glorification (*hitpa'arut*, which shares a root with *tiferet*), because *da'at* is the inner dimension of the *sefirah* of *tiferet*.

The Talmud states that "Any *talmid chacham* (Torah scholar) who does not take revenge and is not vindictive like a snake, is not a *talmid chacham*. On the surface, this seems to completely contradict the Torah directive, "Do not take revenge and do not act vindictively." The explanation is that sometimes, in order to honor the Torah and God, one must take revenge. But that can only be accomplished by a *talmid chacham* who takes revenge and is vindictive like a snake—who doesn't have any personal stake or enjoyment in the revenge, for to him, everything tastes like dust.

Even in the unusual circumstances when one must take revenge for God's honor, it is only permissible when he has no personal enjoyment from it. According to Jewish law, in order to forestall any personal enjoyment, the rabbi should not personally take action. Rather, he should allow his students to carry out the mission, and he should not protest. A true *talmid chacham* who is forced to take revenge or has to glorify himself remains silent, allowing his students to act—while he, like a snake—has no personal benefit from it.

The *Chozeh* of Lublin:
And You Thought You Were Doing Teshuvah?

Rabbi Yaakov Yitzchak Halevi Horovitz, known as the *Chozeh*, or "Seer of Lublin," was born in Poland in 5505 (1745). He was the disciple of the holy Rebbe Shmuel Shmelkeh of Nikolsburg (Mikulov) and the holy Maggid of Mezritch. After they passed away, he became the primary disciple of Rebbe Elimelech of Lizhensk (Leżajsk). He established his chassidic court in the large city of Lublin and the masses flocked to learn Torah from him. The *Chozeh* was known as a holy genius who had the gift of special spiritual sight. It is told that he received this gift from his Rebbe, Rebbe Elimelech. The *Chozeh* was deeply engaged in efforts to bring the redemption. He sent his senior students to spread the teachings of Chassidut throughout Poland and Galicia. Among those students were "The Holy Jew" of Parshischa, Rebbe Uri "the Saraf" of Sterlisk, Rebbe Naftali of Ropschitz and many more. On Simchat Torah 5575 (1814) the *Chozeh* fell from the window of his home under wondrous and mysterious circumstances while he was engaging in spiritual endeavors to bring the redemption. He was severely injured and bedridden for close to a year and passed away on the ninth of Av, 5575 (1815). He was laid to rest in Lublin.

On Yom Kippur, a major part of our prayer service is confession. The following are three stories of confessions—which are an expression of the attribute of *hod* (sincerity) in the soul. These stories are about the Seer of Lublin, and they open a small window for us to understand the mechanism of repentance on a much deeper level.

Story 1: Oops

A Jew entered the Seer of Lublin's chamber with a note upon which his request of the Rebbe was written, as was the custom. There was not a particular request written on the note, simply a request for a blessing for "me and my family." When the Seer read the Hebrew note, he read it with a different set of vowel sounds, so that instead of "for me and my family" the note read, "for me and my son, born to my maidservant." The Jew awkwardly corrected the Rebbe, saying that his request was for him and his family. The Seer re-read the note aloud, making the same "mistake." Once again the Jew corrected the Seer and once again he read the 'mistaken' version. Finally, the Seer said to him, "Wicked man, confess!" At that point, the Jew broke down and confessed that he had indeed sinned and fathered a son from his servant.

Story 2: Just Keeping Clean

A sinner came to the *Chozeh* of Lublin and told him that he wanted to repent. This Jew fell on his face before the *Chozeh*, begging him to help him. When he got up off the floor, the first thing that he did was to spontaneously brush off his clothing from the dust.

Seeing this, the *Chozeh* said that a person like that still cannot repent. In order to repent—especially for sins of sexual impropriety—it is written: "Your garments must be clean at all times." The garments refer to the garments of the soul: thought, speech and action. These garments of the soul must be white and clean. When a person wants to repent for sexual impropriety, but worries about the dust on his pants, it is a sign that he has still not connected deeply to the repentance. power of confession—stemming from his *hod*, his *sefirah* of acknowledgment—has become a destructive force, as is written in the verse in Daniel 10:8).

Story 3: Repentance Diet

A Jew who had already been repentant for a long time came to the *Chozeh*. Before coming to the *Chozeh*, this Jew had taken upon himself all sorts of hardships as part of his service of God. He would fast and do other things to cause himself sorrow, as part of his repentance process. This was in keeping with what is written in musar books, which recommend fasting and other self-initiated hardships to augment the repentance process. (The *Tanya* also writes that one should fast but that this is not the main point. Before the dawn of Chassidut, many opined that these fasts and hardships were the main vehicles of repentance). Although this Jew was already a serious faster and sufferer, he had decided that he should consult with a *tzaddik* about an even loftier service of repentance.

The Jew told the *Chozeh* about his years of fasting and self-imposed hardship, asking the Rebbe to give him a path of repentance. The *Chozeh* answered that this was not the proper path. "If you want me to give you a path to repentance," he said to him, "first you must be physically strong. Without that, you will not be able to bear my path of repentance. Go home and eat and drink well for two months so that you will be strong, and then come back to me."

The penitent went home and followed the *Chozeh's* instructions. For the first time in years, he ate and drank well and indeed got stronger. After a month he returned to the *Chozeh* and reported that he had been eating, drinking and sleeping well and that he felt strong enough to repent. The *Chozeh* told him that it was not enough and that he should return home for another two months of pampering.

The penitent returned to the *Chozeh* two months later. The *Chozeh* looked him up and down and asked him, "Are you ready?"

"Certainly," the penitent answered.

The *Chozeh* was not sure. "I am not sure that you have enough strength," he said. "Are you sure that you are ready?"

"I certainly am," the penitent answered.

"If so," said the *Chozeh*, "let us recite the Confession written in the prayer book together. Repeat after me: *Ashamnu* (We are guilty)."

The penitent barely got the word out of his mouth and promptly fainted. It was not easy to wake him up. When he did wake up, the *Chozeh* said to him, "I told you that you still do not have enough strength to repent. You do not even have the strength to say one word of confession."

* * *

Confession is an expression of the attribute of *hod* (acknowledgement) in the soul, which means submission and confession of the truth. A state of submission in the soul is a prerequisite for confession, but the penitent also needs to recognize his sin (even if it is not an intellectual recognition, but a super-conscious one; the ability to confess one's sins more than once is a sign of an individual's deep recognition of the sin.

In our first story, the Jew knew that he had sinned, but he was not willing to admit it. He simply wanted to ignore the sin and keep going. The *Chozeh* taught him that without admitting the truth, it is impossible to move on. Thus he had to force the confession out of him and spark his submission, which is the first stage of repentance.

In our second story, we meet a sinner who admits his sin. He falls before the Rebbe and asks for a path to repentance. But his spontaneous act of brushing off his pants shows that it was simply lip-service. He did not truly want to admit his sin. It is impossible to truly repent in this manner.

In our third story, the Jew is not only aware of his sin, but he is already is in a state of submission. He is already repenting according to his understanding of penitence, as requiring fasts and other self-inflicted hardships. All of this did not help him to attain true repentance according to Chassidut, because he was still unable to admit his iniquity and say, "We are guilty". He was unable to look his sin in the eye, to truly internalize it.

In order to truly be able to confess our sins, we need a good connection with the *tzaddik*—so that he can guide us to understand what we really did.

When we genuinely admit the truth,—in the merit of the *tzaddik*—the repentance process connects to his power to radiate confession (also stemming from the attribute of *hod*) and acknowledgement to evoke true, deep confession from us. The thoughts we have about ourselves, that we have already attained a high spiritual level, are all purely imaginary. When we recognize the truth—when we look at our true situation in the eye—we can simply faint.

This entire world is known as 'the world of falsehood,' and thus, we tend to lie to ourselves and convince ourselves that we are repenting. In order to stand before the stark truth and say, "We are guilt," we need tremendous spiritual and physical strength. This can only be attained with the merit of the *tzaddik* who will guide us on our path to truth.

The *Chozeh* of Lublin: Sweetening the Severity

One of the greatest disciples of the holy *Chozeh* of Lublin—and some say *the* greatest—was the holy Rebbe Naftali of Ropschitz. Rebbe Naftali had three sons. The custom in those days was to marry off boys at the age of sixteen or seventeen. After the marriage of one of Rebbe Naftali's sons at this young age, his father took him to Lublin, to receive a blessing from the *Chozeh*.

It was customary in Lublin that those seeking a blessing from the *Chozeh* would write the names of the people petitioning for the blessing on a note and would hand it to the Rebbe, without adding any explanation at all. The young groom entered the *Chozeh's* room and handed him his note, upon which he had written his name and the name of his new wife. The Rebbe looked at the note and said two words, "*Nebach, nebach,*" (meaning "How miserable, how miserable," in Yiddish). That did not sound very encouraging. After all, the *Chozeh* of Lublin had spiritual eyes that could see to great depths and distances. If he said, "*Nebach, nebach*"—even repeating it twice—this was reason for concern. The young groom panicked. Who knows what the Rebbe saw for him or his wife? He exited the Seer's room and headed straight to his father, Rebbe Naftali of Ropschitz, who was waiting for him outside the door. The young groom told his father what the *Chozeh* had said.

In Lublin, once the Rebbe gave an answer, it was not deemed proper to repeat the request. In our generation, this was also the case with the Lubavitcher Rebbe. The Rebbe would take exception when someone would receive an answer from him and ask again. Once you ask the Rebbe, you have to accept the answer.

When Rebbe Naftali of Ropschitz heard the worrisome words that his Rebbe, the *Chozeh*, had said, he told his son to immediately return and give the Rebbe the note a second time. The frightened groom entered once again and handed his note to the *Chozeh*. The *Chozeh* looked at it and once again repeated the same chilling words, *"Nebach, nebach."*

Now the situation was even worse. The Rebbe had uttered the same frightening words twice! Rebbe Naftali said that there was no way to leave matters as they were. He instructed his son to enter the Rebbe's room a third time and give him the note one more time. Now the *Chozeh* said to the groom, "Does it not awaken compassion that such a young girl is pregnant with twins? *Nebach, nebach.*"

The young groom exited the *Chozeh's* room and everyone breathed a sigh of relief. This was a joyous announcement, although it could be a challenging time for the young bride.

* * *

This is a story of sweetening harsh judgments.

We can say that at the beginning, the Rebbe saw that the young bride was pregnant with twins and said *"Nebach, nebach,"* about her situation, and ultimately explained what he meant. *chassidim* believe that everything the *tzaddik* says is certainly good, and if this is so, then there is no reason to be frightened from this phrase.

Still, if even Rebbe Naftali of Ropschitz, was so disconcerted by his Rebbe's words that he told his son to return a second and even a third time— then apparently Rebbe Naftali understood that this utterance was indeed severe and required sweetening. Rebbe Naftali did not relent until the *Chozeh* himself sweetened the entire situation.

Perhaps the *Chozeh* saw something undesirable and said *"Nebach, nebach,"* and ultimately sweetened that undesirable situation. Perhaps on an inner level, it was clear to the *Chozeh* from the outset that the compassion-arousing situation was the young girl who was pregnant with twins. But as long as the *Chozeh* did not explicitly say this and sweeten it with his speech, his first utterance could still be a source of severe judgment. Thus it was necessary to return a second and third time with the note until the Rebbe himself said that *"Nebach, nebach"* was simply over the young bride pregnant with twins.

What the Rebbe says when handed a note is a nearly spontaneous reaction. He *Chozeh* what he sees, and what comes out of his mouth as a result of what he sees is spontaneous. Thus, if what he said does not sound positive to the recipient, he has to keep pressing the issue—even urging the Rebbe a bit—until he sweetens his spontaneous remark.

Until the verse, "For God has spoken good upon Israel" Numbers 10:29. is openly revealed through the rebbe's words.

THE *CHOZEH* OF LUBLIN:
THERE IS A JUDGE

Two *chassidim* of the *Chozeh* of the Lublin, who were merchants by trade, visited Lublin to be near their Rebbe. After a few days, they came to take leave of the Seer and receive his blessing for a safe trip.

"Why are you leaving at night?" the *Chozeh* asked. "A person should come at the best time and leave at the best time. It is best to wait until the morning." The *chassidim* explained to their Rebbe that they had an important business meeting and they had to be there on time. The *Chozeh* heard and did not answer.

The two *chassidim* set out on their journey. In the middle of their route through a thick forest, they lost their way. After some wandering, they saw a light from afar—finally—a house in the heart of the forest. The *chassidim* approached the house and to their surprise, saw that there was a Jewish wedding taking place inside. At the head of the table a venerable elder was seated and all the guests sat around the table, but were not dancing as is customary at Jewish weddings. When the *chassidim* asked why they were not dancing, they were told that the guests were all waiting for Reb Moshe the wedding jester to come and tell his jokes. After laughing and merriment, they would get up to dance.

In an instant, Reb Moshe the *badchan* arrived. He stood up on a table and began to tell his jokes. It is customary at Jewish weddings to bring a wedding jester, called a *badchan*, and to pay him substantially—even more than the musicians—for creating a joyous atmosphere for the bride, groom and guests. There were great *tzaddikim* who started out as wedding jesters, such as Rebbe Naftali of Ropschitz and Rebbe Isaac of Homil—the famous Chabad scholar. This is not surprising because in order to tell a truly funny joke, one needs a sharp wit.

Reb Moshe the wedding jester began his repertoire and everyone was joyous and laughing. The guests rose to dance and then, in the middle of the dancing, the ceiling opened, a hand holding a white-hot sword descended from heaven and pierced Reb Moshe the *badchan*'s stomach and threw him off the roof!

The *chassidim* were aghast. When they asked the guests, who were once again seated, what was going on, they answered that they were all waiting for Reb Moshe the *badchan* to come and tell his jokes. After just a moment, Reb Moshe the *badchan* entered again as if nothing had happened, and everything repeated itself. The jokes, the laughter, the dancing and then again the white-hot sword. This happened a number of times.

The *chassidim* understood that they had somehow gotten into a space of impure spiritual beings and that this was apparently Reb Moshe the *badchan*'s punishment. The next time that Reb Moshe entered, the *chassidim* approached him and asked, "Why do you deserve this punishment?

"All my life I was a *badchan*," Reb Moshe answered. "When I would be telling jokes, I would be laughing with the women and joking with them. This is my punishment."

"But tell me," he turned to them, "all the guests here, including the venerable elder, are all impure spiritual beings (called *sheidim*). But you are regular people. Who are you?"

"We are *chassidim* of the Seer of the Lublin. We lost our way and ended up here," the *chassidim* explained.

"Please, I beg you," Reb Moshe beseeched them when he heard that they were *chassidim* of the *Chozeh*. "When you get out of here, go immediately to your Rebbe and beg him to awaken mercy on my soul, so that I can finish my soul's rectification."

The *chassidim* left the house and immediately found themselves on the main road. Instead of going on to their business meeting, they returned to their Rebbe in Lublin and told him the entire story. The *Chozeh* did what he did to rectify Reb Moshe's soul.

"You should know," he said to his *chassidim*, "that there was one reason that I sent you to that place. It was so that you should know that there is judgment in the world and there is a judge."

* * *

This is no standard chassidic story. It is a story full of severe judgment. Indeed, one of the roles of a Rebbe is to infuse the hearts of the Jewish people with the knowledge that the world is not just rolling along by chance. Contrary to the expression that "there is no judgment and no judge," the Rebbe makes it clear that there certainly is. The wedding jester had blemished his service of God by looking at forbidden sights and engaging in sexual impropriety. These two things were perhaps the most essential to the Seer. Thus, apparently, the Seer sent his *chassidim* to see this specific situation so that the fact that there is judgment in this world and there is a judge—reflected in God's attribute of severe judgment—would be deeply engraved on their hearts.

It is written that the heavenly court sits in the Chamber of Merit, which among the seven chambers (*heichalot*) corresponds to the *sefirah* of might, the attribute of judgment. The name of this chamber—the Chamber of Merit— teaches us the purpose of the judgment: To purify the person and give him merit so that he will ultimately be pure and cleansed.

Before the era of the Ba'al Shem Tov, it was customary to learn the book, *Reishit Chochmah*. The chapters in this book in which purgatory is described are so frightening that some of the people who studied them ended up depressed or deranged. Thus, there were *tzaddikim* who forbade the study of this book, particularly the sections that describe the punishments in purgatory. In this story, we find the chassidic approach to teaching the important concept of "there is judgment and there is a judge" and its impacts upon us. There is no need for us to see or imagine the seven vestibules of purgatory. It is quite enough to read this story and take it to heart.

Who especially needs to know that "there is judgment and there is a judge"? Apparently, the merchant who must go out in the middle of the night—not at the best time—to travel to his business meetings. Apparently, those who are sunk in the darkness of this world and its machinations need to know about the cleansing process for those who stray from God. Those people who do not merit to permanently dwell in the chambers of "the light of Torah," where God's presence is clear, need to see the toll of engaging in the mundane world so that they can take it to heart and beware.

RABBI HILLEL OF PARITCH: BREAKING THROUGH THE LIMITS

Rabbi Hillel Halevi of Paritch (Parwich) was born in the town of Khmilnyk in 5555 (1795), to his father Rabbi Meir, who was a Chernobyl *chassid.* In his childhood, Rabbi Hillel was already well-versed in the Talmud and Jewish law, learned books of Kabbalah and prayed according to the intentions of the Ariza"l. It is no wonder that he was called, "the genius of Chemtz," after the town in which he grew up. When he came across the *Tanya,* by the Alter Rebbe, he became an ardent *chassid* of Chabad. Despite all of his efforts, however, he never managed to actually see the Alter Rebbe.

In 5578 (1818), Rabbi Hillel was sent by the Mittler Rebbe [the second Lubavitcher Rebbe] to tens of farming settlements that the Rebbe had established in Kherson, "to sow spirituality and to reap materiality" for the needy. In this way, Rabbi Hillel became the spiritual teacher for tens of thousands of Jews whom he taught and supported. He dedicated his life to disseminating Torah and Chassidut and worked with self-sacrifice to provide kosher food for the Jewish soldiers who had been forcibly drafted into the Czar's army. In 5600 (1840) he became the Rabbi of Paritch in White Russia, near Minsk and then became the Rabbi of the nearby city, Babruysk. Rabbi Hillel would write everything that he heard from his rabbis and add his own explanation. He also composed deep, chassidic melodies. His words of Torah were compiled in the books, *Pelach Harimon, Imrei No'am,* and others. Rabbi Hillel merited a long life and was also a *chassid* of the third Lubavitcher Rebbe, the *Tzemach Tzedek.* He passed away on Shabbat, 11 Av, Shabbat Nahamu 5624 (1864) and is buried in Kherson.

Rabbi Hillel of Paritch, the greatest of the *"oyvdim"* (*chassidim* who perfect the service of the heart in their service of God) of Chabad, made the following observation: "A *misnaged* (one who opposes Chassidut) can be described as "a limit"; a *chassid* is "limitless"; and, a Rebbe is, "the limitless within limits."

* * *

These three stages (thesis-antithesis-synthesis) actually describe a life-process that was common among the chassidic giants—particularly in the early years of Chassidut. In their youth, these *chassidim* were educated according to the ways of the "old world," in what can only be described as a *misnaged* [opposed to Chassidut] type of education that was contracting and limiting. As they grew older, at a certain stage, they rebelled against the limitations and broke through their barriers. This sometimes even included making biting comments against the old ways and rude behavior, which created a scornful backlash among those who kept in line with the traditional ways. To be sure, a certain desire to outsmart the *mitnagdim* was also present in the eyebrow-raising behavior of those early *chassidim*.

Those boundary-breakers who had been educated within the confines of severe limitations and went to the opposite extreme knew (at one point or another) that the ultimate purpose is to reach a balance and to return to the world of limitations while remaining empowered by the limitless. This return was necessary if they wanted to influence the world at large. Such is the transition from a *chassid* to a rebbe. The rebbe is not limited within the confines of the natural world, but does work to infuse those boundaries with God's limitless, infinite light. Even establishing a chassidic court and public movement already creates some limitations on the rebbe's great lights.

In our own times, we can see a certain similarity to those young rebels known as "hilltop youth." These young people were largely educated within the confines of rigid religious and social frameworks and have reacted by rebelling against all limitations with the brash energy of the limitless. They challenge the old frames of mind and world-views and even threaten them. A person with a loving eye and the patience expected from an expert educator can identify the fact that these energies will ultimately endow these youths with leadership abilities that they can employ to positively influence the limited system.

Going back to the founders of Chassidut, it is interesting that both the Ba'al Shem Tov, the founder of Chassidut, and the Alter Rebbe, the founder of Chabad, did not go through this process. They were both born into a natively chassidic approach to life. Orphaned at an early age, the Ba'al Shem Tov wandered through the forests and learned from the hidden *tzaddikim*, the historic precursors to the chassidic leadership. The Alter Rebbe's father and his first teacher educated him according to the principles of Chassidut, even though they did not reveal this to him, according to the instructions of the Ba'al Shem Tov, himself. Thus, instead of beginning with a restrictive and limited approach in their youth and from there breaking out to the limitless, both the Ba'al Shem Tov and the Alter Rebbe began with the limitless and then learned about leading life within the confines of limits.

This is the basis of the Alter Rebbe's advice to the average person, which appears in his book the *Tanya*. The Alter Rebbe realized that most people cannot harmoniously resolve the extremes of boundaries and the unlimited in their lives by becoming Rebbes and synthesizing them at least not until the final redemption. Thus, the Alter Rebbe suggests a different synthesis: Education should be founded on the recognition of God's infinite good and the unlimited power concealed in the soul before its descent into the world. On this backdrop, we identify the boundaries in our lives as originating from the natural inclinations of the animal soul (it is almost impossible for us to be rid of these innate inclinations) and the pervasive heaviness of the world. The synthesis is to employ our limited human energies to uncover the limitless and to nurture it from within the boundaries. The Alter Rebbe teaches us to reveal that we can make a dwelling place for God here in our lower world with every *mitzvah* that we fulfill and with every positive action that we have to force ourselves to take in our limited world.

Breaking down old boundaries is a task delegated to a select few individuals. The majority of people have to learn how to change the world for the better without breaking the boundaries and limits of life. To rectify the world and change our reality, we must slowly but surely employ the energy of the infinite and the limitless within the boundaries of life in this world.

RABBI AHARON OF BELZ: WONDROUS FORESIGHT

Rabbi Aharon Roke'ach of Belz–the fourth Rebbe of the Belz dynasty, was born in Elul 5640 (1880) in Belz (which was in Galicia, Poland at the time and today is in Ukraine). His father, Rabbi Yissachar Dov, was the third Rebbe in the dynasty and his mother, Batya Ruchama, was the granddaughter of Rabbi Aharon of Chernobyl, after whom Rabbi Aharon was named. Growing up, Rabbi Aharon learned Torah from his father and paternal grandfather, Rabbi Yehoshua. Before he was eighteen, he married his cousin, Malkah (who would later be murdered in the Holocaust along with all their children). After his father passed away in 5687 (1927), Rabbi Aharon was appointed to succeed him as the Belzer Rebbe and Chief Rabbi of Belz. Rabbi Aharon was known from a young age for his great holiness, so much so that one of the *tzaddikim* of the generation said regarding him, "Apparently, the evil inclination has forgotten about him." Rabbi Aharon was also known for his great love of Israel and for not being willing to hear anything negative about any Jew, regardless of their level of Torah observance. He said that he was born with the trait of compassion. During the Holocaust, he escaped Poland, where the Nazis were pursuing him personally, first reaching Hungary and then the Land of Israel. After living temporarily in Jerusalem, he made Tel Aviv his home. He married twice more but did not have any children. Rabbi Aharon rebuilt the chassidic sect of Belz in the Holy Land. He passed away on Saturday night, 21 Menachem Av and is buried in *Har Hamenuchot* in Jerusalem.

The first story about Rebbe Aharon was told by Rabbi Mordechai Shmuel Ashkenazi (the previous rabbi of Kfar Chabad).

He related that in 5704 (1944) after the *tzaddik* Rabbi Aharon of Belz managed to escape the clutches of the Nazis (with the help of the Previous Lubavitcher Rebbe) and made *aliyah* to the Holy Land, he stayed for some time with his great-grandfather, Rabbi Shneor Zalman Ashkenazi, one of the elders of Chabad Chassidut in Israel, in his home in the Katamon neighborhood of Jerusalem. Rabbi Aharon asked his host regarding all his family members, and Rabbi Ashkenazi related the details, including details about his son, Rabbi Meir Ashkenazi, who at the time was serving as the rabbi of Shanghai, where many Jewish refugees had fled from blood-soaked Europe. Rabbi Aharon said to his host, "We can assume that this war will end sometime and that your son from Shanghai will come to visit you. If so, please ask him to come to visit me."

Two years later, Rabbi Meir Ashkenazi did come to Israel and, as his father requested, he went to visit the *Tzaddik* from Belz at his home in Tel Aviv. Shortly before that, Rabbi Meir had suffered a stroke, which was visible on his face. Rabbi Aharon noticed this, and said to Rabbi Meir, "True, I am not your Rebbe, but due to my respect for your father's graciousness in hosting me, I have some advice for you. Fulfill the following three recommendations to improve your health: First, do not listen to music. Second, do not eat any dairy. Third, do not visit the graves of *tzaddikim*." Rabbi Meir accepted Rabbi Aharon's advice.

A few years later, when the war was over and the last of the refugees had left Shanghai, Rabbi Meir moved to Crown Heights, NY, home of the Lubavitcher Rebbe and world Chabad headquarters. For an entire year after the passing of the sixth Lubavitcher Rebbe, Rabbi Yosef Yitzchak Schneerson (the Rebbe Rayatz), the Lubavitcher Rebbe refused to fill his father-in-law's role as Rebbe. In those years, the Rebbe was known as the Ramash, a shortening of Rabbi Menachem Schneersohn. When people would turn to him with issues that required the blessing or counsel of a rebbe, the Ramash would send them to the grave of the Rayatz. During that time period, Rabbi Meir came to the Rebbe, with a *pidyon nefesh*, (a written question given by a *chassid* to his Rebbe or a *tzaddik,* usually accompanied by some money to be used for charity). In response, the Ramash told Rabbi Meir, as he did to all those who turned to him then, to go to the grave of the Rebbe Rayatz and pray for the issue that concerned him there. Rabbi Meir, however, told the Ramash that he cannot go to the graves of *tzaddikim*, relating the advice that Rabbi Aharon had given him.

When the Ramash heard his words, his face became very serious and he answered, "The Rebbe of Belz told you that he is not your Rebbe, so you could have asked him about the source of his counsel. But because those words came out of his mouth, we must relate to them with the utmost respect." The Ramash left the room for a moment and returned wearing a chassidic frock and a *gartel* and received the *pidyon nefesh* from Rabbi Meir. This was the first time that the Ramash received someone for *yechidus* (a private audience) as a Rebbe, foreshadowing his imminent official acceptance of the role of Rebbe.

Rabbi Mordechai Shmuel added that when he told this story to one of the Belz *chassidim,* saying that he did not understand the essence of the Belzer Rebbe's advice, the *chassid* told him that he also did not understand all the recommendations, but it was clear to him that the third recommendation—not to go to the graves of *tzaddikim*—was designed, through Rebbe Aharon's wondrous foresight, to bring the Rebbe to the point where he would accept the role of Rebbe upon himself.

* * *

It is written about the Mashiach that he is a "wondrous advisor." This also describes all the true *tzaddikim,* who are an "expansion of Moses in every generation." A true *tzaddik* knows how to identify the essential point of the issue and give good counsel—"a wondrous advisor." The advice of the *tzaddik* comes from his extra measure of understanding (*binah*) and also from his faculty of knowledge (*da'at*) with which he feels the person seeking his advice. The *tzaddik* connects to the person seeking his advice with his faculty of knowledge, while the wondrous counsel comes from his extra measure of understanding, as in the verse in Isaiah (25:1), "Wondrous counsel [comes] from afar with faithfulness and truth." What is the wondrous advice of the Belzer Rebbe in this story? That he foresaw and pre-arranged the situation in which the Lubavitcher Rebbe would have to step into his new role.

The second story about Rebbe Aharon shows his great esteem for the Lubavitcher Rebbe:

As the 19th of Kislev of that year 5711 (1951) approached, before the Rebbe had officially accepted his role as Rebbe, he sent a letter all the chassidic Rebbes and important rabbis of the generation and requested that on the 19th of Kislev, they would hold *farbrengens* in honor of the *yahrtzeit* (day of passing) of the Maggid of Mezritch and the release of the Alter Rebbe from the Czarist prison some 200 years earlier. The Rebbe requested that in their *farbrengens*, the Rebbes would speak about the importance of the study and dissemination of Chassidut and its wellsprings.

Among the recipients of the letter was Rebbe Aharon of Belz, who was considered at that time to be the *tzaddik* of the generation. Rabbi Aharon's assistant opened the letter and read it to him. The assistant, who did not know the new Lubavitcher Rebbe, felt that it was disrespectful of the Rebbe to make a request of the much older Rabbi Aharon. Under his breath, he said in Yiddish, "A young man is telling the Rebbe (Rebbe Aharon) what to do?!" The Belzer Rebbe became very serious and said to him, "You should know that you are playing with fire. Go ritually wash your hands three times and say, 'I regret my words' three times."

* * *

This story is also related in Belz. At the time that this story took place, the Rebbe was still a young man and the Belzer Rebbe was the eldest of the righteous of the generation. The fact that Rebbe Aharon described the insult against the young Torah scholar, the Ramash, as, "playing with fire" was a declaration that this is a *tzaddik* from whose fire we must beware, as is written in *Pirkei Avot*, "Beware [even] their embers."

This story, which endorses the piousness of the Rebbe, refers to the *sefirah* of foundation (*yesod*), "*And a tzaddik is the foundation of the world.*" In Kabbalah it is written that fire comes forth from the foundation, from which we must beware.

Rebbe Dovid'l of Lelov: Childbirth Aid and Spoiled Cholent

Rabbi Dovid Shlomo Tzvi Biderman of Lelov (*Lelów*) also known as Rebbe Dovid'l, was the fourth Rebbe of the Lelov dynasty. He was born to his father Rabbi Elazar Mendel Biderman and his mother, Matel Faigeh, who was the granddaughter of the *Chozeh* of Lublin. From his father's side, he was also a grandson of the Holy Yid. He made *aliyah* to Israel at the age of 6. He married Miriam, who was the great-granddaughter of Rebbe Pinchas Halevi Horowitz, author of the *Sefer Hafla'ah*. Influenced by the Karlin *chassidim* in Jerusalem, Rebbe Dovid'l journeyed to the *"Beis Aharon"* of Karlin. When he returned to Israel, he opened a synagogue for Karlin *chassidim*. After his father's passing, Rebbe Dovid'l refused to become a Rebbe, and it was only after his uncle also passed away that he agreed to lead the *chassidim*. Rebbe Dovid'l was responsible for the money distributed by the Kollel Poland for the Jews living in the Land of Israel, and was even jailed because of the Kollel's debt. He was the head of the yeshivah *Chayei Olam* in Jerusalem and was admired by all the residents of the city–both Jews and non-Jews. He passed away on the fifth of Elul, 1918 and was laid to rest on the Mount of Olives. His son, Rebbe Shimon Nosson Nuta, succeeded him.

The *Ana Beko'ach* Spiritual Remedy

Once a *chassid* whose wife was in the throes of a difficult childbirth (first birth) came to Rebbe Dovid'l of Lelov to ask for a blessing for a successful birth.

Rebbe Dovid'l told him that he should say the "*Ana Beko'ach*" prayer seven times—not too fast and not too slow. The *chassid* entered the room where his wife was giving birth and did exactly as the holy rabbi had instructed him. When he reached the last two words of the prayer, "He Who knows concealed things" (יוֹדֵעַ תַּעֲלוּמוֹת), he already heard the cries of his new baby daughter.

* * *

The initials of the *Ana Beko'ach* prayer spell a Kabbalistic holy Name, known as the Name of 42 Letters. 42 is the value of the word "mother" (אִמָּא). It is a *segulah* (a spiritual remedy) for bringing about a state of, "the mother of children is joyous."[1] When the Israelites encircled Jericho seven times in order to conquer it, they blew the shofars and recited the *Ana Beko'ach* prayer. (Until this very day, *chassidim* and devout people have the custom to encircle places that need to be "conquered" while reciting the *Ana Beko'ach* prayer—particularly with a melody that repeats each word of the prayer seven times). Just as the Name of 42 Letters has the power to open Jericho, which is considered the lock of the Land of Israel, so it has the power to open the womb, described in the Song of Songs as, "a locked garden… a locked spring, a sealed fountain"[2]—when the time has come for the baby to be born.

Rebbe Dovid'l instructed his *chassid* not to recite the prayer too quickly or too slowly. This is the middle road, which is accepted and finds favor in the eyes of God and man. The Alter

---

1.   Psalms 113:9.
2.   Song of Songs 4;13.

Rebbe of Chabad also instructed his followers to do the same when leading communal prayers—not too quickly, not too slowly. This was also the prayer of Chanah, when she asked God for, "offspring of men."[3] The sages explain that she meant that they should be neither too tall nor too short; neither too small nor too fat; neither too white nor too red; neither too smart nor too stupid.[4]

Honoring Shabbat Food

Once Rebbe Dovid'l *spent* Shabbat with his *chassidim* in Meron—burial place of Rabbi Shimon Bar Yochai. A pot of cholent was brought in. The Rebbe said to bring it to him and he ate the entire pot by himself. Afterward, he explained that the fire had gone out from under the pot and the contents of the pot had spoiled. "When they opened the pot, everybody held their nose," he said, "and I could not stand to see how they were shaming the Shabbat food. So I ate it."

* * *

Shabbat is the day that Divinity dwells openly even in the physical world and is present in the food prepared for the holy day. Rebbe Dovid'l's sensitivity toward the Shabbat food is the attribute of the Academy of Hillel, who were careful to honor brides. In a discussion in the Talmud, the Academy of Hillel maintains that even if the bride is crippled or blind, she should still be praised as being, "attractive and righteous." Rebbe

---

3. 1 Samuel 1:11.
4. *Berachot* 31b.

Dovid'l was willing to go to great lengths—and if the reader has ever smelled spoiled cholent, he understands what resolve it takes to eat a pot of it—to maintain the honor of the bride, the holy Shabbat.

RABBI PINCHAS OF KORETZ: INFLATING THE INFORMER

Rabbi Pinchas Shapira, who was known as Rebbe Pinchas of Koretz, was born in Shklow to his father Rabbi Avraham Abba, grandson of the Kabbalist, Rabbi Natan Nata Shapira, author of the book *Megaleh Amukot*. As a son of a Lithuanian, non-chassidic and scholarly family, Rebbe Pinchas studied and delved into the Talmud and Jewish law. From a young age he would write his deep Torah novella in the revealed dimension of the Torah. When the family moved to the chassidic town of Wohlin, his father, who was initially opposed to Chassidut, became familiar with the Ba'al Shem Tov and his teachings and became his student. Rebbe Pinchas followed in his father's footsteps and became one of the Ba'al Shem Tov's most important disciples.

Rebbe Pinchas was famous for his attribute of truth. He once told the Alter Rebbe (who even counted Rebbe Pinchas as one of his mentors, from whom he learned how to serve God) that he worked on his attribute of truth for 21 years. For seven years he worked on recognizing the essence of falsehood, for another seven years he worked to distance any hint of falsehood from himself and for an additional seven years, he toiled to acquire the attribute of truth

Rebbe Pinchas first lived in Koretz and then in Ostraha, serving as a Rebbe in both towns. His famous disciples were Rebbe Baruch of Mezhibuzh (the Ba'al Shem Tov 's grandson, who grew up in his home), Rebbe Refael of Bershid and Rebbe Yaakov Shimshon of Shipitovkah.

All his life, Rebbe Pinchas desired to make *aliyah* to the Land of Israel. At the end of his days, he left Ostraha on his way to Israel.

When he reached Shipitovkah, he became ill and passed away on the tenth of Elul, 5551 (1791). He was buried in Shipitovkah.

Although Rebbe Pinchas wrote a large book in his own handwriting, his descendants had a tradition not to print it. Over the years, a number of anthologies of his teachings were printed. In the past few years, those teachings were compiled in two books titled, *Imrei Pinchas Hashalem*.

There is a wondrous story about Rebbe Pinchas of Koretz, who brought someone close to God in a very original manner, as befits him. It may be said that the greatest transgression in the Torah in our time, and in all times, is informing on a fellow Jew. One may think that the person who worships idols or murders or commits incest is the most evil of sinners. But, according to Jewish law, it is permissible and even a *mitzvah* to use any means necessary to prevent a Jew from informing, be it against a fellow Jew or a fellow Jew's property. The underlying assumption is that the Jew who is being informed upon is actually innocent or that even if guilty, he will be dealt with very harshly because of anti-Semitism.

In the town of Koretz there lived an informer. It is not always easy to neutralize an informer, even though it is permissible and even a *mitzvah* to do so. Generally, these people are well-connected to the authorities, are violent and have personal bodyguards.

The entire town of Koretz suffered at the hands of this informer and nothing could be done to stop him. The chassidic perspective on this fellow was that he could repent and Rebbe Pinchas was sure that this was so. One day, the informer walked past Rebbe Pinchas' window. Rebbe Pinchas called for him to enter his home and the informer, who was a very respectable gent, entered. "I have one request of you," said Rebbe Pinchas. "But I am asking you to promise me up front that you will fulfill my request." Surely the Rebbe wants me to stop informing on my fellow Jews, the informer thought in his heart. That is not something that I can agree to. Not only is it my livelihood, but it is all the enjoyment in my life. It is my very essence. This fellow was addicted to informing on his brothers. Nonetheless, thinking that perhaps the Rebbe had a different request, he decided to take his chances and agreed.

"I see that you are a very important and respectable person," said Rebbe Pinchas. "You should start to don Rabbeinu Tam *tefillin* every morning." In that era, ordinary Jews would only don the *tefillin* made according to the guidelines *of Rashi*, while Rabbeinu Tam *tefillin* were reserved for great rabbis and the pious.

Some time passed and the informer once again passed by Rebbe Pinchas' home. He once again invited him in and once again told him to promise him something and the informer once again agreed. "I see how holy you are becoming," Rebbe Pinchas said to him. "Someone like you will become even more holy if you will take upon yourself to immerse every morning in the mikveh."

"That is fine," the informer agreed once again, and went to the *mikveh* every morning. After that *he* would pray with the *tefillin* of both Rashi and Rabbeinu Tam, and then go to work and inform on his fellow Jews. In the meantime, these positive undertakings had no influence over his behavior whatsoever. He was proud that the *tzaddik* thought so highly of him and instructed him in these holy ways.

Once, the informer had a major victim—a Jew who was apparently evading taxes. Informing upon him would be very lucrative, but our informer had to hurry up and inform on him immediately to the nobleman, who was the local authority. On his way, he realized that he had been in such a rush that he had forgotten to immerse in the *mikveh*. He was passing right by a river, so he decided to jump in and immerse. He was already used to immersing every morning and it was second nature to him. He jumped in the river, ran out, dressed, and did not notice that his long sidelocks and beard (after all, he was a very distinguished Jew) were dripping. He ran with all his files against the Jew into the nobleman's home. The nobleman looked at the dripping informer and thought that he had gone crazy. He threw him out of his home and warned him not to dare to ever return.

* * *

The story does not even relate that the informer repented, but we can assume that he was so ashamed that he did indeed repent. One might argue that all Rebbe Pinchas accomplished was to prevent the informer from informing on his fellow Jews. But presumably, after what happened to him he certainly thought about repenting and we can give him the benefit of the doubt that he actually did mend his ways and return to God.

If so, this is a wondrous way to bring people back to God. Simply to give the most wicked people the feeling that they are pious without even a hint of criticism. It is written that for people who belong to the impure husks—people like Haman—the great honor that Esther gave him was his downfall. The verse in Proverbs (16:18) says, "Before a downfall comes pride." Before a person breaks, he is filled with pride. If we want to break him, we can inflate him until he falls and breaks.

If we are dealing with a Haman, we really do want to break him and let him be hung on the highest gallows. But most people do not need to be hung. They can repent, and this can be accomplished by elevating them spiritually. First, we inflate their egos and when they fall and are shamed, they return to God.

There are many chassidic teachings in praise of being embarrassed. There are even chassidic books that say that the main path to repentance is to be embarrassed. We may have thought that Rebbe Pinchas' plan of action in this story was completely opposed to his attribute of truth. But he had acquired the attribute of truth on its essential level and merited an extra portion of understanding. This gave him the wondrous insight that by inflating the informer's ego, he would actually uncover the Divine spark in his soul—bringing even a Jew who had transgressed the most serious of sins back to the truth.

Rebbe Pinchas of Koretz: Bringing Mashiach Suddenly

Once Rebbe Pinchas of Koretz was staying at a farming village. There was a severe drought and the villagers were literally starving. Rebbe Pinchas was known for his powerful prayers, which were never left unanswered. The villagers were happy that Rebbe Pinchas had come to stay with them and urged him to pray for rain. Rebbe Pinchas went out to the main street of the village and there he beseeched God for blessed rain. While Rebbe Pinchas was still in the middle of his prayers, the skies darkened with clouds and heavy rain poured down on the entire area.

Rebbe Pinchas, who was standing out in the open, was drenched. His students ran out to bring their Rebbe into the dry *Beit Midrash*, where Rebbe Pinchas said to them: "You must be wondering why I chose to pray in the middle of the street and not in the *Beit Midrash*. I certainly could have done that, but if I had prayed in the *Beit Midrash*, the villagers would have thought that I prayed and that after some time, it began raining. They would not have seen that at the moment that I began to pray, God suddenly brought the rain."

"Why is it so important for them to see this?" Rebbe Pinchas concluded. "So that they will understand that this is how Mashiach will come: 'Suddenly the master whom you are seeking will enter his chamber.'"[1]

* * *

This story shows how Rebbe Pinchas focused all his efforts to hasten and bring about the coming of Mashiach. Even when praying for rain that the world needs in order to survive—and Rebbe Pinchas does want to give the world what it needs—he acts to infuse the world with Messianic consciousness. In order for people to be in awe of the suddenness of his action and learn that the redemption will come in the same manner, he was even willing to endure a major soaking. As the Lubavitcher Rebbe said, we have to "live with Mashiach." This does not mean that we should abandon other necessary activities, but rather, that we should connect everything to the ultimate purpose of bringing Mashiach.

This story is very characteristic of Rebbe Pinchas, who was known for his attribute of truth, upon which he worked all his life and which he imparted to his disciples. Rebbe Pinchas showed the villagers the power of true prayer. When one prays from the point of truth, then "His word runs very swiftly."[2]

Chassidut teaches that truth is on the middle axis of the sefirot. When we merit to connect with the middle axis, things happen without delay. As the Lubavitcher Rebbe would say, "truly promptly and immediately" (תֵּכֶף וּמִיָּד מַמָּשׁ). The Rebbe

---

1. Malachi 3:1.
2. Psalms 147:15.

said that if we would truly pray and beseech God, crying out, "Until when???" with all our hearts, then at that moment, immediately, the Mashiach would come, as is written, "God is close to all those who call Him, to all who call Him in truth."[3] This is the point that Rebbe Pinchas wanted to teach. It is an important point, connected to the Lubavitcher Rebbe's directive "to live with Mashiach" and to the action we must take to bring the Mashiach.

There is something distinctly beautiful about the word "suddenly" (פִּתְאֹם). Suddenness or immediacy draws *down* directly from the *sefirah* of crown. Something that happens suddenly is a surprise, surprises originate in the soul's super-conscious, the *sefirah* of crown. The *sefirot* below crown, the intellectual, emotive and behavioral *sefirot* are part of the conscious soul, where there are no surprises. It is only from the power of the super-conscious crown that sudden surprises are generated.

The service of 'suddenness' is the service of *teshuvah*, repentance. When we have a thought of true repentance, we can change ourselves even "in one hour and in one moment," all the way from being a consummately evil person to being a consummately righteous person. This is the awakening from below that draws down the sudden revelation of Mashiach from Above, as Maimonides (the man of truth) determined: "Ultimately, Israel, at the end of their exile will repent and they will immediately be redeemed."[4]

Our heads have to be programmed so that whatever we do, we will bring the Mashiach 'suddenly', in one moment. In order to make this obvious to everyone, we have to be willing to stand out in the rain and get a good soaking.

3.   Psalms 145:
4.   Maimonides, Laws of Repentance 7:5.

Rabbi Simcha Bunim of Peshischa: Do You See What I See?

Rabbi Simcha Bunim Bonhardt of Peshischa *(Przysucha)* was a disciple of The Holy Jew. Both were disciples of the *Chozeh* of Lublin. Rebbe Bunim was known for his great wisdom, and his first rebbe, the *Chozeh* of Lublin, said about him in Yiddish, *"Er is meiner chochom,"* "He is my wise man." The *Chozeh* of Lublin had 120 very great students. Each of them was a *tzaddik* and all of them became rebbes in their own right. Yet, from amongst all of those *tzaddikim*, the Seer of Lublin called Rebbe Simcha Bunim alone, "my wise man." Rebbe Bunim was very wise and very happy as well, as indicated by his name, 'Simcha.' He passed away on 12 El*ul,* *5587* (1827).

* * *

Every *tzaddik* has his own way of doing things. For the Seder n*ight on* Passover, there were *tzaddikim* who would invite many guests and some who would invite fewer. Rebbe Bunim would invite only a few of his most special students for his Seder. Thousands of *chassidim* would come to Peshischa for Passover, but it was forbidden for them to come to Rebbe Bunim's Seder. The Rebbe himself would arrange places for all of his *chassidim,* so that they would have a place to stay and eat with a family in the village. All the *chassidim* would pray together and hear Rebbe

Bunim's words of Torah together. But the rule was that if you were not invited to the Rebbe's Seder, you would not come.

One of the regular *chassidim*, who was not invited to the Rebbe's Seder, went to the family that the Rebbe had arranged to host him. He saw that they were in great distress. They very much wanted to host him, they said, but they literally had no food for him. Even for themselves, they just barely had the required amount of *matzah*, and if they would include him, there would not be enough to go around.

Soon it would be nightfall, and the *chassid* had nowhere to go. With no choices, he went to one of the greatest disciples of Rebbe Bunim—Rebbe Yitzchak of Vorke (the founder of the Vorke and Amshinov dynasties), crying to him that he had nowhere to go for the Seder. "I will do you a great favor," Rebbe Yitzchak said to him. "Even though it seems like it is against the will of the Rebbe—I will take you with me. I will bring you to the Rebbe's table and you will sit with me. But there is one condition. You must not say a word. You must sit in silence from the beginning of the Seder until the end. Do not ask any questions. If you accept this condition, I will bring you with me."

The *chassid* has no choice and it was also a golden opportunity, by Divine Providence, for him to attend the Rebbe's Seder, something that only the privileged few merited. "Yes, of course, I agree to your condition," he answered Rebbe Yitzchak.

Our *chassid* entered Rebbe Bunim's home and sat in silence behind Rebbe Yitzchak of Vorke, as if he was not there at all. The Seder went along uneventfully, until they reached the section, near the end, where Elijah the Prophet is invited to enter. When they opened the door for Elijah, somebody actually did enter. He seemed like a very simple farmer. The farmer went over to the Rebbe and began speaking with him about all sorts of mundane matters: the crops, the wheat in the fields and more. This went on for a long time. An absolutely mundane conversation. Try as he could to remain silent, our *chassid* couldn't keep his composure. He turned to Rebbe Yitzchak and asked. "Who is this man, with whom the Rebbe is conducting such a long mundane conversation?"

"Shhhh!" Rebbe Yitzchak responded. "You are here on the condition that you do not speak and that you do not ask any questions about what you see. But as long as you asked, I will tell you one thing: You see one person, I see somebody else and the Rebbe sees somebody entirely different."

* * *

What do we learn from this story? The uninitiated see the farmer as a simple man, with nothing special about him. But the great disciple, Rebbe Yitzchak of Vorke, says that he sees someone else and that when the Rebbe looks at him, he sees someone entirely different.

Some people judge others according to their external appearance. They think that what they see on the surface is all there is to the person. Actually, they are judging them according to their bodies or garments. Other people go deeper. They can see the soul and when they speak with someone, they are not looking at his body, but at his soul. Then there is a third type of person, a true rebbe, who sees not only the soul but the soul root. Every person has a soul root, "An actual part of God Above," in the words of the Tanya. They can see how this person is connected at his root all the way to God's Absolute Essence. This is the aspect of "the soul of souls" seen by a Rebbe.

Our story does not tell us who the farmer was. But if we judge by his timing, he could very well have been Elijah the Prophet. What we can learn from this is that when we look at someone, we must not dwell on our first impression, which is very superficial and says little, if anything about the person. If we merit and learn much Torah, we will be able to see the person's soul. Whoever will be a Rebbe—and the Lubavitcher Rebbe said that in our generation everyone can be a Rebbe—can see something entirely different. He can see the other person's soul root.

This is a beautiful story about Rebbe Bunim of Peshischa, which exemplifies his wisdom. He was the wisest of all the *tzaddikim* of his time. A wise person of the impure husks can only see superficial things, but the penetrating eyes of a truly wise person learned in the Torah, sees the soul. And the Rebbe can even see a person's soul root, the very essence of the soul.

Rebbe Yechiel Michel of Zlotshov: Abundant Charity

Rebbe Yechiel Michel of Zlotshov (Zolochiv), called "The Maggid of Zlotshov" was born in 5486 (1736) to his father, Rabbi Yitzchak of Drohovitch (Drohobych). Rabbi Yitzchak was initially opposed to the Ba'al Shem Tov, but subsequently became one of his admirers and sent his son, Yechiel Michel, to learn from him. Rebbe Michel composed wondrous chassidic melodies, the most famous of which is called "Awakening Great Compassion." When the Ba'al Shem Tov passed away, he asked his disciples to sing this melody and then promised that any person—no matter where he may be—who would sing this melody with a great awakening for repentance—he, the Ba'al Shem Tov—would join him in his song and would awaken God's great compassion upon him.

Rebbe Yechiel Michel was the first of the chassidic *tzaddikim* who delayed the morning prayers, saying, "Just like the tribe of Dan, which would march at the rear of the camp of Israel and gather all the lost belongings, so I gather all the misplaced prayers that were uttered without proper intention and uplift them to their source."

Most of his life, Rebbe Yechiel Michel lived in great poverty, becoming wealthy only at the end of his life. He then said that wealth broadens one's consciousness to serve God. He was famous as a talented orator and was a maggid in the towns of Brody, Kalk, Zlotshov and Yampol. He was a maggid in Zlotshov until he passed away and was buried in Yampol on the 25th of Elul, 5546 (1786).

When Rebbe Yechiel Michel of Zlotshov married, his new father-in-law gave him an immense dowry—1000 golden coins. Rebbe Michel originally thought that he would invest the money and earn his livelihood from the profits, while continuing with his intense Torah study and service of God. But he immediately had a second thought: If he would have assured income for all his life, what would be of his trust in God on a daily basis? Thus, on second thought, he decided that he would give half of his dowry to charity. That was a huge sum of money, similar to someone giving one million dollars to charity in our times.

Rebbe Michel wrote out an advertisement and publicized it throughout the city, stating that every poor person was invited to come and receive a generous donation. Word traveled quickly and all the poor people showed up on Rebbe Michel's doorstep. Rebbe Michel joyously handed out large sums of money to all the people. Not one person was left out.

Now Rebbe Michel began thinking again. What about the second half? "What do I need it for?" he asked himself. "Surely I can live very well for my entire life with just half of this half. Where is my trust in God?"

Once again Rebbe Michel announced that he would be giving donations to all in need. Once again, all the poor people came and received hefty donations.

Rebbe Michel repeated this until the entire dowry was gone. All that he saved for himself was one cow. He had a small barn behind his house where he kept his cow. At least he and his family would be able to have some milk every morning from the cow.

But then Rebbe Michel contemplated some more. "Where is my trust in God?" he asked himself. Rebbe Michel called the ritual slaughterer to slaughter his cow. Then he distributed the meat to the poor. The next morning his wife went to milk the cow and was faced with an empty barn. "Where is the cow?" she asked. "She went up to heaven," Rebbe Michel answered. "And what will we eat?" she persisted. "God will help us," Rebbe Michel assured her and his righteous wife accepted his words.

Some time later, a poor bride came to Rebbe Michel, crying that she had absolutely no money for wedding expenses—not even for a wedding gown. Rebbe Michel approached his wife, who had only one nice dress and asked her to give it to the poor bride. His wife agreed. We see that in a marriage, all blessing comes from the wife. She could have become quite upset over how Rebbe Michel managed their funds but she was right behind him—despite the fact that it was her father who had given them this immense sum of money.

After his wife gave the poor bride her only dress, she sat down and sewed herself a dress from a burlap sack. We don't know how long she had to wear the burlap dress until she was able to buy a new dress, but that is what she did. This is quite an amazing story about Rebbe Michel of Zlotshov's wife.

More than this story is about Rebbe Michel's attribute of trust in God, its inner dimension is about his love of Israel, giving everything that he owned to charity.

* * *

Charity During Elul and the High Holidays

In the Tanya, it is written that the directive of the sages that one's own life takes precedence over someone else's life is only in the situation discussed in the Talmud, where there is enough water for only one person to survive. In that particular case, one is instructed to keep his water for himself and not share it with another person. But if one encounters a poor person and his own life is not in danger, he is instructed to give generously. If the poor person does not have enough food to feed his family, while I have food in plenty, I am obligated to give him the food that was for my family, according to the poor family's needs. This is how the Alter Rebbe of Chabad explained the obligation of charity.

In the Tanya (Epistle 17), the Alter Rebbe expounds on the verse in Psalms, "Your *mitzvah* is very broad." He explains that this broad mitzvah is giving charity. God performs this mitzvah of giving charity on a constant basis. He gives us life and sustains us and the world at every moment. Likewise, when we give charity, we are treading the path of Abraham, who performed acts of charity throughout his life. When we give charity, we create an infinitely broad vessel for the revelation of God's transcendent light in our lives. The Alter Rebbe explains that the principle from this charity remains intact for us for the future days to come.

In essence, the Alter Rebbe's entire epistle is about charity. According to the order of the Tanya daily study portion determined by the Rebbe Rayatz, we learn about charity just before *Rosh Hashanah.* The high point of giving charity, according to the Arizal, is the eve of *Sukkot.* But during the entire time period from Elul, through to *Rosh Hashanah, Yom Kippur* and *Hoshanah Rabbah,* we must give generously and in abundance.

MORE BOOKS BY RABBI GINSBURGH

GENERAL

What You Need to Know About Kabbalah

190 pages

The Wondering Jew

Mystical Musings &
Inspirational Insights
284 pages

The Inner Dimension

Insight into the Weekly
Torah Portion
405 pages

Kabbalah and Meditation for the Nations

216 pages

The Hebrew Letters

Channels of
Creative Consciousness
502 pages

SCIENCE AND MATHEMATICS

913: The Secret Wisdom of Genesis

160 pages

The Breath of Life

Torah, Intelligent
Design and Evolution
186 pages

137: The Riddle of Creation

400 pages

Lectures on Torah and Modern Physics

184 pages

Wisdom: Integrating Torah and Science

216 pages

The Torah of Life

Nutrition + Nervous System
44 pages

LEADERSHIP

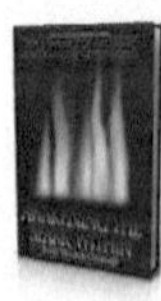

Awakening the Spark Within

Five Dynamics of Leadership
that can Change the World
200 pages

Rectifying the State of Israel

230 pages

RAISING A JEWISH FAMILY

Consciousness and Choice

Finding Your Soulmate
284 pages

The Art of Education

Internalizing Ever-
New Horizons
302 pages

The Mystery of Marriage

How to Find True Love and
Happiness in Married Life
500 pages

PSYCHOLOGY AND MEDITATION

Anatomy of the Soul

144 pages

Transforming Darkness into Light

Kabbalah and Psychology
192 pages

Living in Divine Space

Kabbalah and Meditation
288 pages

A Sense of the Supernatural

Interpretation of Dreams and
Paranormal Experiences
208 pages

Frames of Mind

Motivation According
to Kabbalah
256 pages

HEALTH AND YOUTHFULNESS

Body, Mind and Soul

Kabbalah on Human
Physiology, Disease
and Healing
342 pages

The Twinkle in Your Eye

Kabbalistic Remedies for
Preserving Youth and Memory
202 pages

In honor of our dear friend, a benevolent man of
good deeds and charity,

Chaim Tzvi Nash

in honor of his birthday.

"Happy is the man who has made God his trust."
(Psalms 40:5)